T0287479

MAD DOG

GRAVESEN

MAD DOG
GRAVESEN

The Last of the Modern Footballing Mavericks

CHRIS SWEENEY

First published by Pitch Publishing, 2019

Pitch Publishing
A2 Yeoman Gate
Yeoman Way
Worthing
Sussex
BN13 3QZ
www.pitchpublishing.co.uk
info@pitchpublishing.co.uk

ISBN 978-1-78531-485-8

Typesetting and origination by Pitch Publishing
Printed and bound in India by Replika Press Pvt. Ltd.

Contents

To Thomas

You might never read this, nor ever want to.

But I salute you.

You did it and did it your way.

I hope any kid out there from any walk of life who feels the need to conform and tone things down uses you as an inspiration.

Never lose your identity.

Stand up tall.

Prologue

Wednesday, 9 March 2005.

ZLATAN Ibrahimović was revelling in the electric atmosphere under the floodlights of Turin's Stadio delle Alpi along with a host of superstars of world football such as Zinedine Zidane, David Beckham, Ronaldo, Lilian Thuram and Alessandro Del Piero.

The eyes of the world were on the titanic clash, with a host of subplots and intrigue. Bars, homes and diners across the globe were tuned in watching two heavyweights go toe to toe, slugging it out until one would rise victorious.

It was football at the highest level: fast, skilful, tactical and performed by the finest exponents of the game.

Within a microcosm of this epic tussle, Zlatan — known for his tremendous ego and self-belief — decided to indulge the watching millions with some of his signature impudence.

He found himself isolated, one on one with a Real Madrid player near the corner flag. The giant Swede swayed his hips looking to put his opponent off balance, then darted forward like a tiger, slipping the ball through the defender's legs.

A nutmeg in a game of this magnitude is the ultimate putdown, designed to make an opponent look stupid. No professional wants to get done like that in front of the watching world.

As Zlatan did it, he expected the Real Madrid player to wince, realising he'd been make to look like a stooge, while the Swede galloped on to collect the ball to a flurry of shrieks from his adoring public.

But what he didn't bank on was the guy whose dignity he'd just stripped had not being raised at one of Europe's most glamorous, opulent clubs. He hadn't been cosseted and groomed for stardom in a flash academy, where promising teenagers are treated as if they are African kings.

He was dealing with a man who comes from a place most of the planet has never heard of. A place with a rock-solid code of representing yourself with pride and dignity, a code that's ingrained into all of their folk.

Everyone there — the Danish town of Vejle — knew what was coming next.

Zlatan never got the ball. The other guy didn't buckle.

He turned around and showed the big Swede, 'You might be chasing the flash of cameras but I'm here to win, lad.'

It was style over substance. The Real Madrid player?

His picture is on the cover of this book — and this is his story.

Introduction

I
T'S no small undertaking deciding to write any book, no matter what the subject or genre is. But working on a topic that is rich and unmined are the deciding elements that tip the scales. When you discover that sweet spot as a writer, the juices start flowing and your mind begins racing. You wonder where you could take things — and what you could manufacture from the plentiful raw materials that are flashing before your eyes.

That was the case with this book. Although we shared a city for 12 months of his career, I never came across Thomas Gravesen or had any reason to pay him much attention, apart from the fact he was a well-known footballer I'd seen on television down the years.

But I began hearing whispers and noticing snippets about this character, who seemed to be cut from a different cloth. Whenever I dropped his name into conversation, people either lit up and regaled some tale they couldn't believe was true, or they'd say nothing apart from vaguely remembering him. I also noticed that any mention of him online seemed to attract a lot of interest, and that those who knew the real Thomas were desperate to find out more. It was clear the affection Thomas was held in by those who've encountered him at close quarters. There's a lot of mystery. Very little is known about Thomas by ordinary fans and the general public, even though he was one of the most interesting and unusual players of his generation.

Here was a character who had the makings of being the subject of a riveting book. He was a rich, successful footballer, but his story resonates beyond sport. The more research I did, the more I could see that Thomas had gone through experiences that everyone could relate to.

Thomas is a person who's lived a dream. It's a phrase bandied about in the current climate of reality TV as things are handed to people, without any achievement. But very few individuals ever truly realise it and actually do what they've always imagined in their mind's eye. To aim for a goal and reach it.

Every one of us, regardless of our standing, has dreams but the truth is that most of us will never see them fulfilled. It's the beauty of life. It's what gets us up every morning. You might get there, then again you might not. But we all keep going, hoping that one day it might be us that's lucky enough to join that small, select group of people who turn those dreams into reality. Thomas did that.

Normally, with this type of book, the subject collaborates, allowing you to take a shortcut directly into their mind and raid their memory bank. I explored that option but Thomas is a difficult person to contact. He has no website or social media. Even tracking down which country he lived in wasn't easy. The avid interest in him means there's more than one red herring out there, causing even more confusion. I did approach one person who purported to be his agent but that turned out to be an erroneous claim. Eventually, I managed to get to someone close to him but was informed that he wouldn't even consider any proposal.

As I began to collate more research and speak to sources, I realised that Thomas was an even more interesting subject than I'd previously thought and, in fact, this book would be better without his involvement. It's the old cliché of someone boasting about how out-of-the-ordinary they are. If they have to say it themselves, then it's a false proclamation. Someone who's a true one-off doesn't need to mention it. Ironically, as an author, I have to admit that actions can speak louder than words.

Thomas has a certain unexplainable charisma and anyone who's had dealings with him remembers him vividly as a larger-than-life character but at the same time sensitive and naïve. He has an uncanny ability to leave a mark, whether it's through football or his outlandish personality. Lots of phrases like 'screwball', 'loose cannon', 'madman', 'barmy', 'unicorn', 'mental' and 'lunatic' have all been used to refer to him, but in a positive sense. Put simply, he's a man you never forget.

More often than not, Thomas had a wide smile plastered across his face, a glint of devilment in his eyes and was clearly revelling in living his dream. The ex-team-mates I've spoken to all recalled how bubbly he was. Thomas has an infectious vibe that all of them still look back on fondly. To them, that lived longer than anything he ever did with a ball.

And that's the crux of this book. It's about someone who lived a dream but was then ultimately robbed of his childlike enjoyment of it in cruel circumstances. It's about how he took a talent, applied it and succeeded by going all the way to the top of the world of football, and back down again.

It was a journey full of achievement, media scandals, controversy, mystery, intriguing rumours and sublime skills, but the person on the journey did it in the only way they knew how — with honesty and integrity.

There are few more powerful things in life than watching someone truly happy and motivated to do something, purely for the joy it brings them.

We only get one shot at life. Thankfully, some like Thomas make the most of it. And for the rest of us, it's never too late to be inspired to do so.

Chapter 1

Money, Money, Money

NOTHING stays the same and nowhere is it more true than in professional football.

It's the world's game, played by all creeds and colours, from the Brazilians honing their samba skills on sun-drenched golden beaches, to the Germans developing technical skills in training centres to the South African youngsters playing barefoot and carefree in the townships. It's that universality that has seen the game change so much.

Decades ago, players developed at their own pace. They were signed by clubs and given coaching as youths, but had to complete an apprenticeship to see if they would be lucky enough to be afforded a career in the game. Now it's far more sophisticated. The hopefuls are honed for the professional game with sports science, personalised training and genetic studies whilst still children.

Take the world's two best players. Lionel Messi left Argentina for Barcelona's academy aged 13, taking his family with him. Cristiano Ronaldo was reared by Sporting Lisbon and played for their first team at just 17. Hours and hours were put into their development. They and today's generation of players were raised to be footballers. It's gone so far that talented children under ten now change clubs for a transfer fee and teams establish academies in far-flung countries all across the world hoping to spot — and claim — a diamond in the rough before a rival does.

Of course it's worth it or they wouldn't bother. Portuguese club Benfica reported in 2018 that they'd earned £230 million by selling their own academy graduates over a three-year spell. With the club's academies becoming more vital and with the players joining so young, the pressure to churn out consistently good footballers is ever present. That has caused the desired end goal to become far narrower; there's no tolerance for anything other than what is deemed to be the 'consummate professional'. This book celebrates a player who would likely never have made it through that sort of regimented academy system.

These developments have been fuelled by the rapid improvement of communication via the internet and satellites, which has given every team the chance to attract a global audience. Our hunger for and reliance on live games is reflected by the huge cost of broadcasting rights. For example, in the 2018 round of English Premier League deals, Sky paid £3.57 billion and BT £885 million. Only three years previously, the league pulled in a staggering £5.14 billion for the rights to screen games. But when the league began in 1992, the price for 300 games for a five-year period was a relatively paltry £191 million.

Manchester United, who many regard as the world's most famous club, attracted their first sponsor in 1982 in electronics giant Sharp. It was followed by financial juggernauts Vodafone, AIG, Aon and one of the largest car manufacturers, Chevrolet. But things didn't stop there. Manchester United have led the way and now have an official airline partner (Aeroflot), an official feature film partner (20th Century Fox), a global online marketplace partner (Aladdin Street), an official tyre partner (Apollo) and, among others, even a global wine partner (Casillero del Diablo).

Real Madrid, European football's most successful team, have a similar stack of deals. They use the term 'main sponsors' for Emirates and Adidas, and have global sponsors in Movistar, Microsoft, Nivea Men, Audi, Hankook, Manou, Exness and EA Sports.

Even the great Barcelona aren't above this 'bun fight'. Despite their motto *'Més que un club'* (More than a club) and counting the Pope among their season ticket holders, they conceded defeat after proudly refusing to allow any sponsors to sully their iconic shirts. Initially, they had the UNICEF logo and donated money to the fund annually. But they signed with the Qatar Foundation in 2011 before moving on to Qatar Airways and currently display Japanese online shopping behemoth Rakuten.

Clubs have even started selling the names of their stadiums. Germany's best-known team Bayern Munich used to play in the city's towering Olympiastadion, built for the 1972 Olympics. But when it needed remodelling, Bayern moved to the cutting-edge Allianz Arena, named after the German financial services firm.

Smaller clubs jumped on this trend, with Scottish outfit Livingston attracting the ire of some of their fans by renaming their stadium The Tony Macaroni Arena, after a low-end Italian restaurant chain.

It wasn't long before moguls and billionaire tycoons started buying clubs as moneymakers. The earliest to raise eyebrows was Russian Roman Abramovich, who bought Chelsea for £140 million through his private investment company Millhouse in 2003. He spent more on numerous big-name players, which won the club English Premier League titles and ultimately European football's biggest prize, the Champions League. This success meant revenue shot up, and companies had to pay significantly more to be aligned with Chelsea.

Since then, there has been a flood of rich individuals wanting to acquire blue chip teams. The world's most valuable club, according to Deloitte's 2018 report, is

Manchester United, earning €676 million. They are still owned by the American Glazer family, who assumed control in a takeover which valued the club at $1.5 billion in 2005. By 2018, that had shot up to $2.3 billion.

Manchester City was bought by former Thailand prime minister Thaksin Shinawatra before Abu Dhabi's deputy prime minister Sheikh Mansour bin Zayed Al Nahyan usurped him. The list of clubs bought by tycoons is a who's who of the game. AC Milan was owned by Chinese businessman Yonghong Li's Rossoneri Sport Investment before American billionaire Paul Singer's Elliott Management Corporation took over. Paris Saint-Germin belongs to Qatar Sports Investments and Singaporean billionaire Peter Lim snapped up Valencia.

The one constant that hasn't changed is the reliance on the players to deliver success. But there's no longer merely an expectation. There's now a necessity driven by the pressure of such vast sums.

No one wants to deal with loose cannons. They get short shrift because the number of youngsters wanting to make it is so abundant. The message is: 'Either toe the party line or you're out the door.'

It's the reason why off-the-cuff characters like Eric Cantona and George Best aren't around any more. Another is maverick Faustino Asprilla, who missed the 1993 European Cup Winners' Cup Final for Parma after a bus driver hit his car. The irate Colombian striker ended up on the bus, so the driver trapped him but didn't bank on Asprilla shattering the windscreen with his feet to escape. Then there was wildman Paolo Di Canio, who described a winning goal as 'like having sex with Madonna'. He also shoved a referee on his backside and made fascist salutes to celebrate goals.

Today's footballers aren't like that. Instead, they roll off a cookie-cutter production line. That's not to say they aren't skilful, dedicated athletes, but the characters are the ones fans idolise — the players whose names kids put on their replica shirts.

It's not just in football, either. Kimi 'The Iceman' Räikkönen is the most popular Formula 1 driver even though he's racing with skilled multiple world champions Lewis Hamilton and Sebastian Vettel. Fans adore Kimi's character; he says very little but refuses to adhere to the PC line.

We live in a time when we've become spoiled for sporting excellence. What sets some apart is their innate DNA, the way they think, the manner in which they do things. Usain Bolt was the reason every continent tuned in during the Olympics. They wanted to see if the great man could break another world record. Everyone knows his Lightning Bolt celebration but before his races the Jamaican would joke with the mascot kids while his rivals could barely blink and were springing five feet in the air with nervous tension.

There's no rhyme or reason to it. We're all wired differently. You can't fake it — that's the beauty of being a maverick.

One of the issues this book deals with is how the vast sums of money have influenced the way football has developed. One-off extroverts that excite the masses are a thing of the past. Footballer Stuart Pearce built a reputation at semi-professional club Wealdstone FC while working as an electrician before jumping into the pro ranks, going on to win cups with Nottingham Forest and appearing for England at the World Cup. Stuart says, 'The modern game is so sanitised and exposed to the media that it almost suppresses personality.'

Look at how Paul Gascoigne prepared for the biggest game of his career, the semi-final at the Italia 90 World Cup in front of a global audience of tens of millions. Instead of resting up or being sequestered in his room, Gazza endured a full-paced five-set game of tennis in the sweltering Sardinian sunshine with an unwitting holidaymaker at the team hotel, only hours before kick-off. It wasn't the best preparation, but it's what he felt like doing. Now professionals wouldn't be allowed to act like that. They would have to accept the decision on how they spend their rest time being made for them.

This book turns the spotlight on a man who's been described as a grenade with the pin pulled out, the last of the real mavericks to make it through to the pinnacle of football intact. A guy who even the erstwhile Baddest Man on the Planet, Mike Tyson, saluted as being impressively out of control.

A man who went from his small hometown team to the most glamorous and prestigious club side of all time, leaving behind a reputation that's still marvelled at and a cult following everywhere he's been.

His name is Thomas Gravesen.

Chapter 2

A Star is Born

VEJLE is a small, cosy town located on the south-east of Denmark's Jutland Peninsula, one of Scandinavia's most picturesque spots. It's surrounded by lush green forested hills, has a charming harbour and boasts an iconic windmill, which dates from 1847 and is now a tourist attraction showcasing the town's history of milling. It's also not far from the headquarters of Lego, the legendary toy company.

Nearby is another town called Daugård, which is sleepy, charming and even smaller. It's near the coast and offers a picture-postcard view of the Vejle Fjord, which ring-fences an idyllic stretch of calm water. It's rarely been on the radar of the wider world, apart from holidaymakers looking for a relaxing spot to escape the rat race.

That's where Thomas Gravesen is from. He is the town's most famous son, the only other native of note being rapper

Tue Track. Thomas was born in 1976, the eldest son of Georg and Jette-Marie, who also had a younger boy, Peter. Thomas arrived in March, so was born under the Pisces star sign that predicts that they will be 'very focused on their inner journey' which, for all the Zodiac naysayers, is eerily accurate when retroactively applied to Thomas.

He couldn't have timed his arrival any better from a football point of view. The following year, Vejle's most famous export, Allan Simonsen, was banging in goals for fun for Borussia Mönchengladbach in Germany's Bundesliga and even helped them reach the European Cup Final. They lost to the mighty Liverpool but only after he opened the scoring. That year, the great and the good of European football competed for the prestigious title of the continent's best player. It came down to three; Simonsen, Kevin Keegan of the aforementioned Liverpool and French genius Michel Platini. Simonsen narrowly won the most votes and was handed the honour that later became known as the Ballon d'Or, a major achievement for someone hailing from a small nation that didn't feature heavily on the international scene.

That summer, Simonsen left a comfortable set-up in Germany to jump in at the deep end with Barcelona. The plucky Dane lasted three years at the Nou Camp, hitting double figures in goals every season. In fact, the main reason he left was the arrival of a certain Diego Maradona, meaning Barcelona had one too many foreign players under league rules. With Maradona and temperamental midfielder Bernd Schuster, known as the Blond Angel, picked as the two who would play in the starting 11, Simonsen agitated to leave for a club where his talents would be given greater prominence. Oddly, he moved to south London side Charlton Athletic but left after three months as the club couldn't afford to keep paying his wages, which wouldn't have been inconsequential as Simonsen had rejected Real Madrid and Tottenham Hotspur to join the English minnows.

Amid all the turmoil, Simonsen decided to return home to what he knew and joined his local team Vejle Boldklub, whom he'd originally played for before leaving to seek fame and fortune. The fans and town were in raptures with their prodigal son and best footballer coming home, and for youngsters like Thomas it must have been a magical time. The local guy who'd been crowned Europe's best player and scored goals in the continent's most famous stadiums was now back amongst them.

The Simonsen effect worked wonders and transformed the club, even though he was injured and didn't play during the 1984 season. The furore drove the squad on and they won the Danish league, their fifth league title and, at the time of writing, their last trophy. Considering the club formed back in 1891, it was a monumental time to be a Vejle fan.

Aged eight, Thomas was in the perfect place to soak it all up. He was watching his heroes in their red and white shirts humble the more successful Danish sides of previous years, such as Akademisk Boldklub and Kjøbenhavns Boldklub. You can imagine him sitting transfixed, watching his idols parading about in a blaze of glory under the inspiration of this heralded Danish forward who'd gone on to conquer the upper echelons of the game, and in the process become a bona fide superstar. It was a time for a young, impressionable kid to realise that anything was possible.

Another of Vejle's heroes, Ulrik le Fevre, brought the curtain down on a distinguished career as an elegant left-winger, known for his cannonball shot. He won the Bundesliga with Borussia Mönchengladbach at a time when German football was a dominant global power. West Germany were European champions in 1972 and added the World Cup two years later while Bayern Munich were Europe's premier team with icons like Franz Beckenbauer, Gerd Müller, Paul Breitner and Uli Hoeness. But still, it was le Fevre who won the first-ever goal of the season. He went on to lift a hat-trick of league titles in Belgium with Club Brugge and came home to Vejle, inspiring them to win the Danish title in 1978.

Simonsen's trajectory mirrored that of le Fevre, who honed his skills at Vejle, left and put himself on the football map, before coming home to pass the torch to future stars from the same sleepy corner of Denmark. Another who did the same was Johnny Hansen, a cultured defender, who left Vejle for 1. FC Nürnberg and then became part of that epic Bayern Munich team the ruled Europe. He then came home to Vej4le and was part of the same squad as le Fevre that won the league in 1978.

The fact that three very well-known, successful stars did that proves just what sort of club and town Vejle is. It's renowned for looking after its own and has a strong sense of community. Everyone is raised to respect where they come from and fly their flag with pride. Even now, if you were to go to Vejle's games or cruise around the town, you'd have a decent chance of seeing these stars of yesteryear. Theirs is a community whose bond is stronger than fame and fortune.

Then Thomas had a stroke of luck. Back in those days, despite some players making it to big teams and winning trophies, they didn't earn the staggering sums that players do today. Most of them had to find work as although they left the game with a decent sum and savings, it was not enough to cover them for the rest of their days. After retiring, le Fevre became a maths teacher at the high school in Vejle. One of his students was a lively young man by the name of Thomas Gravesen. He was 14 and spent three years in le Fevre's class. The ex-footballer says: 'In the rankings, he was not the first, he was in the middle, but he was always the first when there was playing time — out with the ball in his hand and he played football all the time. He was also the last who came in after playtime. He was crazy about football and he still is crazy about football.'

The young lad's skills didn't go unnoticed by his teacher, who'd watched Thomas and recognised that he had something special. He might not have been the best at long division but he was a cut above when it came to splitting a defence with a perfect pass. It was clear to the retired star that they had something special on their hands and potentially the next one to roll off their production line. They all seemed to be players with class, skill and a certain flair – Vejle does not produce kick-it-and-run merchants.

Later in his career, Thomas was asked about his early days as a schoolboy. 'I just played football all the time,' he recalled. Initially living in Daugård, his dad would take him to training but the youngster had a steely determination to make it in the game, so he moved to Vejle, where he was able to focus even more on what he enjoyed most.

Another thunderbolt then hit Danish football when Thomas was 16 and dreaming of a career in the game. The country of less than six million took on all-comers and against all the odds won the 1992 European Championships in neighbouring Sweden. Yugoslavia had qualified but were booted out by the game's ruling body after the break-up that followed a bitter civil war. As the Danes were runners-up in the Yugoslavs' group, they were promoted at less than a week's notice. The squad had to be scrambled from the beaches where they were topping up their tans on their summer holidays.

Denmark earned a goalless draw with England in their opening match and built up momentum from there, eventually reaching the final after a nail-biting battle with the Dutch that went to penalties, with the great Marco Van Basten the only player not to convert his spot kick. Germany were heavily fancied to win the final as they could now call on players from both east and west after reunification. Their team featured the likes of Jürgen Kohler, Matthias Sammer and Jürgen Klinsmann, but Denmark stunned them, winning 2-0.

Thomas must have been enthralled by what he saw and had already become an avid reader and collector of magazines. He was fascinated to find out the names of the players and their histories. A tiny nation like Denmark winning one of the game's biggest prizes spurred him on even more.

In another serendipitous move, le Fevre then started back at Vejle as the youth team coach and now had Thomas under his command, but this time not in the classroom. The one thing that really stuck out for le Fevre was Thomas's committed attitude and laser-beam focus. It didn't matter if it was a light training session or a full-blooded match, he gave it 100 per cent all the time. There was no in between. He only had one mode. Ulrik said: 'At that time, he had a high fighting spirit, he was always fighting. Even if it wasn't a serious game, he was fighting, fighting, fighting but he was such a good technical player. I had a very good team. Five of them went into the first team the next year.'

The highly praised quintet consisted of Thomas, Kaspar Dalgas, Alex Nørlund, Jesper Søgaard and Peter Graulund, but ironically the best of the lot was the last to get a contract. Thomas saw his four team-mates sign deals while he was left out in the cold — or so it appeared. At the time, it was thought the club were worried that he was just too much of a maverick and wouldn't be able to temper his volatile personality or learn how to channel it. Actually, Thomas credited being the last to get a contract as another factor that drove him on. 'It also meant that I wanted it a lot more,' he admitted.

Not only did the young guns move up, le Fevre went with them, joining the first-team squad as assistant manager under boss Ole Fritsen. He was a legendary figure at Vejle, another former player who had three different spells as manager. By the time Thomas joined the squad, he was in his final stint after taking the job on again in 1994. At the start of the 1995/96 season, Fritsen realised he had a squad that could go places, mainly thanks to the promising and talented players that le Fevre had brought through. But it wasn't going to be easy. They had the ability but would need to be drilled and taught how to use it.

To Fritsen, it was clear that Thomas was the standout and the two formed an unbreakable bond. He is referred to by Thomas as his mentor. Speaking about the great man and realising that he had been a difficult customer in his early years, Thomas said: 'He trusted and believed 100 per cent in me and he spent much of his energy to make me a better football player. I can only thank him for that because if I had not gotten the right coach at the right time, they would have given up with me. Ole had been a top player, so I listened a lot.'

Sadly, Fritsen passed away in 2008 so I was unable to get his memories of that time, but he had previously spoken about Thomas, telling Vice Sports, 'Sometimes I would send him off in training because he was so fanatical that he was constantly yelling at his team-mates and making gestures as if he were about to break their legs.'

Morten Pelch, who works in Vejle's communications department, also knew both men and lifted the lid on how Fritsen got to grips with his rampaging midfielder, who would sometimes boil over and let anger cloud his judgement. Morten said: 'He taught him a trick where he had to imagine he had three stones in one pocket and when he got angry, he taught him to remove the stones and put them in the other pocket, so he didn't lose his temper. Fritsen said he [Thomas] was the complete footballer. He had excellent technique, a good physique, stamina — it was only his temper that was the problem. But as he got older you didn't see it as much [although] of course he still had some incidents.' Thomas admitted to using the three-stone mind trick all the way through his career.

Even Thomas concedes that he could be a handful as a youngster. He said, 'I did not really respect the others at all. It was just me. And if it was not just me, I became completely hysterical.'

Fritsen clearly knew what he was dealing with, which was a very skilful player but one who needed unique handling. He had so much to offer but it would have to be unlocked in a precise and delicate manner. Morten added, 'Thomas was supposed to get his debut earlier when he was younger but because he went in so hard on someone in training, Fritsen said he shouldn't be rewarded for that, so it took another six months before he actually got the chance. When he was playing youth football, you could see he had the will and technique. We could all see his ability and skill.'

Evidently, it was very much a carrot-and-stick approach, which connected with Thomas's unique character. Wily old foxes Fritsen and le Fevre knew how to guide him. The opening game of that league season saw Vejle host Brondby, with 8,218 fans packing into the stadium eager to get their first look at their bright new team full of home-grown talent. The youngsters acquitted themselves well but went down 3-1 to their more experienced opponents. The game was marred by an incident after Brondby's second goal, when celebrating supporters were crushed against a barrier that gave way and snapped. Twenty-four fans had to be taken to hospital but no one was seriously hurt.

As the season wore on, Thomas flourished on the pitch and became the team's leader. The players all looked to the 20-year-old for their direction. Thomas didn't actually wear the captain's armband but was skipper in everything but name. He would demand the ball, burst through tackles and drive up the pitch like a rampaging bull. He was head and shoulders above the standard of the Danish league, even at that age.

But his volatile temperament was still there and it let him down on occasions, most notably during a 1-0 home defeat to Aarhus Gymnastikforening (AGF). Thomas was shown a straight red card, scuppering his team's hopes of getting back on level terms. He was raw, an unpolished diamond.

The team were playing with flair but, like Thomas, their lack of nous was sometimes allowing games to slip away. They finished the season in the bottom half of the league but put down a marker for the next campaign when they thumped Ikast FS 5-0 in a devastating display in their final home game at the end of May. They might have been lacking a little know-how, but they could play.

It was in Thomas's second season — 1996/97 — that he really began to make an impact. The team got off to another shaky start as they went down 3-2 away to AGF. But it was clear to everyone that Thomas had become an even better player and was still developing. He was now fully dictating games. Fritsen had moulded him into a skilful, powerful sweeper, who could stride out of defence and control the tempo. It's hard for someone so young to be the fulcrum as it requires not only confidence but also ability, and the other players have to take a back seat and follow their conductor's lead.

It was the guidance from Fritsen that allowed Thomas to do this and channel his almost frenzied focus. He'd snap into challenges, win the ball and then come powering up the field looking to build an attack. He was like a Scud missile that needed direction to do his best work, and the old masters Fritsen and le Fevre were more than able to furnish him with the coordinates.

Chapter 3

Graduation Day

T HE first home game of the new season confirmed what so many pundits were expecting of this young team as they thrashed Odense 4-0. More wins followed, including a highlight performance against big guns FC Copenhagen, who were dispatched 3-0 in October. The fresh-faced youngsters kept it going, winning more than they lost.

Thomas played his final league game for his beloved Vejle in front of their home fans in June 1997 as his second season came to a close. He didn't know it then, but he would say goodbye in the best possible manner by scoring the game's opener after only two minutes. The team went on to win 4-0.

With Thomas putting in all-action performances, Vejle were a class apart and finished that season in second spot. They were runners-up to Brondby, who had far more resources at their disposal. The reason Vejle won the hearts and minds of the neutrals during those two years was their style. They played attacking, carefree football. They were a bunch of young guys playing for the love of the game and enjoying themselves doing it. The second-place finish meant they qualified for the UEFA Cup and Fritsen was named manager of the year. Thomas also ended up as joint top scorer, which was no mean feat for a sweeper and underlined how good an all-round player he was becoming.

Part of Vejle's success was down to their more professional approach off the field. During the build-up to games, Fritsen made it mandatory that they spend all day together, preparing and resting as a unit, which fostered a strong team ethic. But this boisterous gang, led by the fun-loving Thomas, had lots of energy so they'd pretend to rest but instead go into the club's indoor hall and play frenetic five-a-side games in their club suits. They didn't worry about injury. Even after matches, they'd have the ball out again in the shower room, playing keepy-uppy and smacking it off the button to turn the water on. Their own madcap rules meant they weren't allowed to use their hands.

While he was very much one of the young crew, Thomas struck up another bond that would last his entire career — and still exists today — with John Sivebæk. He was another of Vejle's graduates who went on to Manchester United, Saint-Étienne and Monaco amongst others before making the familiar journey home. Thomas respected the playing influence of the veteran, who had been part of Denmark's European Championship-winning team in 1992 and became protective of the wild youngster. The bond was such that Sivebæk became Thomas's agent and looked after him throughout his career, and to some degree, still does today. I reached out to John during my research in the hope that he could offer an insight into Thomas, but in one text message he labelled me disrespectful for writing this book. Many years later, Thomas spoke about their partnership. 'I'm concentrating on playing soccer, and that's how we split it up,' he said: 'I take care of the sports and John's got the business.'

It was also around this time that Thomas's uniqueness began to seep out. Before, he'd just been a game-for-a-laugh youngster. But as he became an adult, it was clear he had a character that was different from all the other players. In one of his early-career interviews, Thomas told how he took a job at a workshop that sold spare car parts because he needed something on which to focus his pulsating and consuming energy when he wasn't playing. He said: 'I need to know that the alarm clock rings in the morning, otherwise I will never go to bed. Previously, I had a period of three to four months where I did not work. I only slept in the morning and could not sleep at night. I switched completely night and day and could clearly notice that my game was getting worse and my condition worse.'

After explaining the issue to the club and Fritsen, Thomas got some support and was able to revert to 'just' being one of European football's best young players. But it showed he had an almost abnormally obsessive personality that was to become more prevalent once he left the comfort of his homeland behind. It would be national news in any major country like England, Italy or Spain if a young star was combining their career with a regular job as a salesman in a spare parts shop.

The squad driven by Gravesen under the tutelage of Fritsen and le Fevre gave the town of Vejle back its pride. They'd gone back to basics and showed they had the heart, desire and most importantly the ability to represent their hometown club. There is nothing sweeter for a football fan than seeing home-grown talent flourish. Not even a megastar who joins for a fortune will make a supporter happier than when they see one of their own doing it. It's part of the game's tribal nature and had Vejle's fans smiling and singing as they watched their swashbuckling heroes play the kind of football usually reserved for video games. They probably knew most of the players' families or had seen them around the town when they were teenagers. Now here they were as a Danish version of the Manchester United team dubbed Fergie's Fledglings, which included former youth players Ryan Giggs, David Beckham, the Neville brothers Gary and Phil, Nicky Butt and Paul Scholes, all of whom went on to be ranked among the best players of their generation.

But unlike in Manchester, there was no room to grow. Vejle couldn't attract crowds above 10,000 simply because there weren't enough people in the town. They were never going to be competing for the game's big prizes. But the scouts around Europe had heard about the wonderful things happening at Vejle and most of all about an all-action midfield maestro called Thomas Gravesen. They knew he had skill but had also heard reports that he could be overly aggressive. Although he was only 21 at the time, he looked older. He was muscular, well built, had slicked-back light brown hair and large hooped earrings in both lobes. Even in pictures, you could see the smouldering intensity in his eyes. This was someone who had drive and determination, and clearly believed that he had something to offer. He wasn't just knocking on the door, he was kicking it down.

Everyone knew it in Vejle. Thomas was going to be the next local talent to venture into the world of high-stakes football and represent the small, sleepy town. Morten Pelch said: 'He's one of our own, we're so proud of him. He's the last legend we had. After the 1997 season, we had a lot of turmoil and hard years, so when the people think of him they think of the good era. We won games, the stadium was full and Thomas was a big part of that.' Le Fevre echoed those sentiments, confessing, 'I'm very proud and we're all proud of him in Vejle.'

So after 58 league games and ten goals across two stunning seasons, a still young and raw Thomas was flying the nest — and going with the best wishes of everyone around him. But none of them could have anticipated just what an impact he'd make and how far he would go.

Before his departure, he had one final challenge to meet — making his European debut. Vejle were drawn against Israeli outfit Hapoel Petah Tikva in the UEFA Cup qualifying rounds. The young Danes earned a goalless draw in the home leg, and narrowly lost the return 1-0 in the sweltering summer conditions.

And that was it. Thomas left his beloved club on a high. The real tragedy was that unlike so many of Vejle's heroes, he would not come back. The fans would never see him pull on that red and white shirt he cherished so much again. The man who would soon become known as 'Mad Dog' was now off the leash. One of his friends, fellow midfielder Jesper Mikkelsen, who was part of the same dazzling team, put it best when he said: 'Thomas had a winning mentality and madness that led him beyond us.'

Chapter 4

Deutschland
über alles

THOMAS clearly meant business by the time of the move in August 1997. His hair had been cropped and the earrings had gone. His destination was Hamburger SV in exchange for 1.5 million Deutschmarks. They hadn't been the only major European club to make a move; Serie A giants Napoli had come in and offered him a deal to go to Italy.

He wasn't interested. In classic Gravesen style, he said forthrightly, 'I wanted to play in the Bundesliga. Here I have the best perspective to become a full international. What do I want in Naples? I can go on holiday there.' As the Italian fans who watched a peak Diego Maradona play in the city would no doubt agree, Naples was more than merely a holiday destination.

Apart from his jewellery, Thomas didn't have to change much as HSV were known as 'Die Rothosen' (The Red Shorts) and played in a similar kit to his beloved Vejle. But it was a massive leap for a 21-year-old who only had two seasons of professional experience under his belt.

Hamburg is Germany's second-biggest city, famous for its lively Reeperbahn district and also a hotbed for football. It plays host to two city rivals, HSV and St Pauli. HSV played at the intimidating 62,000-capacity Volksparkstadion, which has since been significantly modernised. When Thomas arrived, it was an old-school arena that generated a cacophony of noise. Not only was it a massive jump in terms of profile, with more fans now coming to his games than lived in Thomas's home town, it was also a quantum leap in the level of competition. Back at Vejle, he'd been so dominant that he was far better than both his team-mates and opponents. At Hamburg, he would need to go up a level and prove himself all over again.

The squad was one of serious quality. It included skilful Croatian defender Josip Šimunic, energetic wide midfielder Hasan Salihamidžić, who went on to win the Champions League with Bayern Munich and was later a star for Juventus, top-class keeper Hans-Jörg Butt and dynamic centre-forward Tony Yeboah, who British fans will remember for his unforgettable volley while playing for Leeds United, which is still talked about more than 20 years later. Thomas was handed the number two jersey and slotted into defence. In the eyes of manager Frank Pagelsdorf, who was also new at the club, he was viewed more as someone to shore up the back line with licence to bring the ball up the pitch, rather than as a midfielder.

Despite Thomas's youth, Pagelsdorf immediately saw him as one of the squad's key players. As HSV had paid serious money for him, he was not there to learn his trade. They were banking on Thomas as one of their main men. Pagelsdorf raved, 'We have watched him seven times. He embodies the absolute will to win in every bit of play. He is great in the air and takes the term "challenge" literally. An opponent can at times remain on the ground after one of his tackles. Thomas isn't arriving as a talent with us. For me, he immediately becomes one of our leaders.' That was a clear statement that big things were already expected of Thomas.

It wasn't all positive, though. Pagelsdorf soon had his first run-in with Thomas over how the player addressed him. In Germany, there are two ways of referring to people: the familiar 'du' or the formal 'sie', which is more polite and respectful. Thomas went with the former whenever he spoke to his new boss, which ruffled a few feathers and was met with the stern reply: 'No. Call me Mr Pagelsdorf or trainer.'

Being unused to Thomas, it wasn't long before Pagelsdorf began to get frustrated with his tactical indiscipline. He would go on the pitch and without realising it be so consumed by the game that he'd start charging all over the place in search of the ball. Without the guidance of Fritsen or le Fevre, Thomas was out of control. But even allowing for this, he played in all but eight league games that season, which was no mean feat considering German football was in such a good place. The national team had won Euro '96 and Borussia Dortmund lifted the Champions League the following season. But for HSV, the season overall was a major disappointment. At times they even flirted with relegation before finally finding some form in the spring to finish in ninth place.

Thomas instantly won over the fans as they lapped up his bone-crushing tackles and pure commitment. He'd brought the same intensity he'd shown at Vejle and hadn't been intimidated by the reality of playing at a higher level. A video clip of the young Dane running along the front of the crowd at a training session, touching their hands as they cheered wildly, showed Thomas had something the fans identified with. This was long before social media, so players and supporters could only connect in the flesh.

The irony was that Thomas had been one of the fans himself. An avid HSV follower growing up, as part of his obsessive nature he'd collected their matchday programmes for seven years. He knew all about the league as he'd been reading German football magazine *Kicker* for the same length of time. So yet another piece of the puzzle seemed to slot into place for him. Thomas was almost a fan out there on the pitch, which endeared him to the crowd even more.

Nothing summed that up better than a sign on the buzzer outside his apartment in Hamburg. Thomas put up a written slogan saying 'Gravesen HSV' just in case anyone was passing and wanted to chat about how the season was going. Nowadays social media provides a direct link with fans but back then being able to ring one of your star players' buzzers was properly opening up the communication channels. Today, any modern footballer giving out their address, never mind advertising it on their buzzer, would be an alien concept as many top players live in gated communities with security patrols. Not Thomas. Anyone was welcome to stroll up and chew the fat. Due to things like this, the German fans adopted him as a cult hero and he was given the nickname 'Humörbombe' for his larger-than-life personality.

It was also Hamburg that sparked Thomas's massive interest in Audi, the car manufacturer. He noticed them being driven a lot in Germany and began to take a shine to them, a love he never lost. While most players his age would be fixing their gaze on a Ferrari or a Hummer, Thomas was interested in fuel economy. He really liked what he'd heard about the company's diesel engine. In fact, it was something that was so deeply ingrained in him, he was still telling his team-mates about it in his last few professional seasons. It was light hearted but this again showed how Thomas had almost tunnel vision. Once he was into something, that was it, he was in — hook, line and sinker. The car obsession was something that astounded his team-mates everywhere and became even more random as his spending power increased.

But it wasn't only four-wheelers that he had an interest in. Thomas also had a motorbike, which was hardly the most sensible mode of transport for a professional footballer travelling around a busy city. All clubs harbour a fear of seeing their prized assets shatter their limbs or get injured and today's young pros are part of such tight regimes that they wouldn't even consider it.

It was only thanks to HSV team-mate Bernd Hollerbach that Thomas was rumbled. Defender Hollerbach had a reputation for driving very fast in his Porsche, ignoring any speed limits where they were in place as Germany's Autobahn allows drivers to go as fast as they like in some parts.

A club insider revealed how one day Hollerbach arrived at HSV's training ground looking crestfallen but also with an expression of shock on his face. The source said, 'He'd been speeding as usual, overtaking everyone, when out of nowhere a biker flew past him doing 160mph. The rider was clinging on for dear life dressed in a t-shirt, shorts and flip-flops but his identity was hidden under a helmet.' The tale goes that with a shake of the head, Hollerbach sighed, 'The bloke must have had a screw loose.' It was only when he got inside to change for training that he spotted Thomas standing there in a t-shirt, shorts and flip-flops. It was him who'd been riding the bike! He was casually getting ready, thinking nothing of it, and went out for the day's session leaving Hollerbach dumbfounded.

Chapter 5

Tick, Tick, Boom!

T HE 1998/1999 season began poorly for Hamburg as they drew 1-1 away to FC Nürnberg. But despite the team's inconsistent performances, Thomas had attracted the attention of Denmark coach Bo Johansson, who called him up to the national squad for the first time. The team were going through a transitional period but were still led by their inspirational goalkeeper Peter Schmeichel. Thomas had showed his class in the training sessions, so was named in the starting 11 for the friendly against the Czech Republic.

Johansson had seen Thomas play for Vejle so knew he wasn't just a defender. He put him in midfield but the game ended in defeat for the Danes, with Thomas hauled off half an hour from the end. What Johansson didn't know was how intense Thomas was. Once he had something in his mind, that was it. He'd struggle to hold his position and roamed the pitch desperate to get on the ball.

That, along with his crazy antics, was still kept mainly behind closed doors. It meant fans and the general public had yet to discover what Thomas was really like. The first impression even led a puzzled Johansson to speak to the media and question if Thomas was 'psychologically stable'.

Thomas had also made an explosive impression at HSV, striking up a bond with fellow Dane Allan Jepsen, who was a fringe player in the squad. Thomas told Jepsen that he had some 'special fireworks' and that it would be great fun to set them off on one of the outdoor training pitches. Jepsen didn't see the harm in it, so he went along as Thomas dug out a mound of earth and instructed Allan to light the fuses. As he did, he saw Thomas sprint away furiously into the distance. It was only when Thomas shouted back, telling Jepsen to drop them and run, that his friend fled in a panic. Within seconds, an almighty boom left a huge crater in the ground. Thomas's fireworks were certainly 'special'. They contained real dynamite.

On the pitch, Hamburg suddenly exploded themselves as they beat defending champions FC Kaiserslautern then took the scalp of big guns Borussia Dortmund. Thomas was playing well but again his focus began to wander as he had been given a limited role. Pagelsdorf started leaving him out as his frustration grew. It's impossible to correlate that with the team's results but they began to tail off before Thomas was brought back in and the squad pulled together to deliver a six-game unbeaten run, finishing the season in seventh place.

Thomas's erratic form meant that Johansson had lost faith in his ability to fit into the Denmark team, who were bidding to qualify for Euro 2000. Thomas had been in the first 11 for their opening qualifier against Belarus before being taken off, then came on as a substitute in the next match, which they lost 2-1 to Wales. Apart from a friendly appearance against Croatia, Thomas would not play any part in helping his country make the finals. Why? Johansson couldn't relate or get through to him, and without the right approach he couldn't unlock the young maverick, who was definitely good enough to have played in that team. Squad member Morten Wieghorst, who scored one of the most vital goals of the campaign against Italy in Naples, setting Denmark on their way to a 3-2 victory, offered his view from inside the camp. 'They were two sides to him [Gravesen]. Thomas wanted to be the best he could be, he always did things 100 per cent. He'd stay behind after training to improve, he worked a lot on his finishing and his passing was phenomenal. Thomas could hit it 50, 60 yards with real precision.'

There's a cliché that goes 'every soul is a diamond and it takes a trained eye to see and appreciate it'. While Johansson was an experienced manager, he'd never played at the highest level. The other Danish players knew how good Thomas was, even though he was much younger and less experienced than most of them. They could see his class but

Johansson couldn't see the wood for the trees. He'd banished Thomas because he wouldn't fit rigidly into his system. But Thomas's all-consuming drive was always going to make that impossible. Wieghorst added, 'He was a total one-off. Thomas was a dynamic midfielder. He was the kind of player who'd disappear from his area and then show up in dangerous areas for the opposition. It was [in] those areas he could really do his best work, so to get the best out of him and for the team, you had to have a manager or a head coach who appreciated the importance of finding the balance. You wouldn't have been able to have two players like Thomas in midfield, that would go wrong. Basically, it's like that with all the good players. They're so good at doing their thing but to make them fit in a team, you need balance and you need someone else to do the other type of work.'

Now he had a much higher profile, the media started to take an interest in Thomas's antics. His obsession with cars was the first thing that saw him appear outside the sports pages as Danish journalists found out that he'd bought 14 cars in less than four years. But in true Thomas fashion, he didn't buy them all at once. He'd just wake up one morning, decide he was bored of his car, then go and buy another. There was no rhyme or reason to what he'd turn up in. He would just buy whatever was in his mind that day and not worry about what anyone else thought.

The fans were also hearing about his unique character by this point and, as such, he'd become a cult hero. They loved that this crazy Danish guy had a pool table at home emblazoned in the team's colours, with the club crest on the felt. Again, it became an obsession. Thomas would play pool for hours on end and, as everything he did, it was all or nothing. That's why he was such a good footballer but at the same time he had become a loose cannon that Hamburg's management team were losing patience with.

The same club insider recounted another bizarre incident in which Thomas and partner-in-crime Allan Jepsen decided to have a laugh one afternoon. They covered the entire wellness area at the team's training base in foam, soap and shampoo, so it became their own personal giant, infinity-style swimming pool made of bubbles. The pair got naked and began sliding through the whole building all the way to the swimming pool, where they launched in by doing cannonballs. A member of staff was alerted and came in to catch the young Danes having the time of their lives. Their only punishment was to clean the place up before the manager saw it.

The club then discovered that Thomas wasn't just using the motorbike for high-speed dashes to training. He was actually going home to Vejle most days of the week. One way, the journey is 175 miles and usually takes around three hours, but speed freak Thomas was doing it in well under two. He'd leave training, go home, and then come back for the next session. It underlined just how much energy Thomas had and with no one there to rein him in, he was spending his days driving like a maniac back to the small, sleepy town where he felt most at ease. It was another example of the contrast with footballers his age, most of whom would go to designer shops in the afternoons and then hit the nightclubs.

The start of his third season, 1999/2000, was a pivotal time for Thomas and it's no understatement to say that the next few months paved the way for his eventual move to the best club side of all time, Real Madrid. One huge part of that was his girlfriend Gitte Pedersen. They'd got together as teenagers back in Vejle and she was also a footballer. She'd completed her studies, graduated and moved to join him in Hamburg, working in a kindergarten and also playing for Hamburg Ladies. It meant Thomas's daily rides to Vejle were no longer necessary as she'd been the main attraction.

Her being in Germany seemed to increase Thomas's focus as he started the year out of the team. Pagelsdorf could basically no longer tolerate or control him. He was fuming at the number of yellow cards Thomas had collected for his bone-crunching tackles, many of which weren't needed. Thomas only had one mode, on his motorbike or off it, which was full throttle.

Pagelsdorf had already grown tired of reminding players not to use mobile phones on the team bus when he'd look back and see Thomas happily chatting away. When he blew the whistle to end training, Thomas would totally disregard it and just carry on shooting at goal while the other players huddled around the coach for a briefing. Thomas wasn't doing it to challenge his manager or to show disrespect; he just saw things differently in all aspects of life. His close friend from Vejle, Kaspar Dalgas, came to see him in Hamburg and realised that without the trusted duo Fritsen and le Fevre, Thomas was on the road to destruction. Kaspar said, 'Thomas always mentions Ole as the best coach he has had. That's probably because he was allowed some things that others did not. In Germany, it became more dull and he was struggling to get involved. That's why it came to battles with Pagelsdorf. Thomas's behaviour cost him sometimes.'

With some wise words from people in his inner circle, Thomas turned things around. Soon, he was back in the team. His ability was never the issue; it was only the manic way he did things. It ended up being his best season and Hamburg shot up the table, finishing third and qualifying for the Champions League. It was thanks in no small part to Thomas and his surging runs, which opposition players couldn't handle. He was stronger and more skilful than most players he faced, so he could beat them for power or use a little trick. He had plenty in his arsenal. Commenting on this upsurge in form, Pagelsdorf explained, 'There are two reasons. For one, Gravesen has recognised the seriousness of the situation. He wants to join the squad of the Danish national team for the European Championship, which will take place this summer in Belgium and the Netherlands. But that will succeed only if he fights for a place at HSV. On the other hand, Gravesen seems to have realised that with all his extroversion, he is only a part of the whole, the team.' That was Thomas in a nutshell: give him a target and he'll hit it.

German football journalist Mark Lovell said, 'The HSV fans remember Gravesen with a special fondness. He was a maverick. He was someone who always gave 110 per cent for Hamburg. It was also when footballers were allowed to have a little bit of character; they were not just faceless marketing machines. He always had a glint in his eye and fans definitely appreciate that.'

Johansson was in the same boat. He couldn't fail to notice how good Thomas was any longer, despite the fact Gravesen hadn't played for Denmark since the first two qualifiers and had missed the play-offs, in which the Danes smashed Israel 8-0. Thomas was named in the squad for Euro 2000 and handed the number 20 jersey. Now the entire continent was going to get its first look at one of the game's only true mavericks, and he wasn't going to let them down — on or off the pitch.

Chapter 6
Toffee Time

BELIGUM and the Netherlands hosted Euro 2000. It is still regarded as one of the highest quality tournaments by many football writers, as some of the game's greats faced off against each other.

Romania were conducted by genius Gheorghe Hagi. England were represented by their so-called golden generation of Beckham, Sol Campbell, Steven Gerrard, Michael Owen and Paul Scholes. Italy were strong with Alessandro Del Piero in their number 10 shirt alongside dominating captain Paolo Maldini, mesmerising defender Fabio Cannavaro and goal machine Filippo Inzaghi. Sweden had inspirational striker Henrik Larsson, Spain brought Raul, Pep Guardiola and Fernando Hierro while Yugoslavia had silky skipper Dragan Stojković marshalling their midfield. Denmark went into the tournament as the lowest ranked team apart from Slovenia and to put the cherry on the cake, they ended up in Group D, which lived up to its Group of Death nickname.

They were in with the French, who at the time were the most exciting team on the planet after storming to an epic World Cup victory on home soil two years earlier. In their ranks were the imperious Zinedine Zidane, flying machine Thierry Henry, powerhouse Lilian Thuram, man mountain Marcel Desailly and other household names such as Nicolas Anelka, Patrick Vieira and Didier Deschamps.

Also in Group D were hosts the Netherlands, who were full of class acts too, including Clarence Seedorf, Dennis Bergkamp and Jaap Stam. The other team was the Czech Republic, who were no slouches either with Pavel Nedvěd, Patrik Berger and Vladimir Šmicer in their ranks.

This was going to be mission impossible for the Danes. They had a solid squad but no superstars and only the top two qualified for the knockout stages. For those who knew Thomas, this would be exactly the sort of situation in which he would thrive. Stack the odds against him, give him a challenge and he will do everything he physically can to conquer it.

Denmark kicked off in Bruges against France, whose strength was so frightening that well-regarded operators like Dugarry, Trezeguet, Pires and Karembeu were only on the bench. Things went according to the script as Les Bleus took the lead thanks to skipper Laurent Blanc. Henry then added a second. Denmark boss Johansson realised they could be in for a hiding, so after 72 minutes he rang the changes and Thomas came off the bench to enter the fray. Right away, it was clear he was up for the fight, regardless of the score. He thundered about the pitch and raised the tempo. Wiltord added a third but Thomas had laid down a marker. He could face Deschamps, Zidane and Vieira, who were all in their prime, head on and compete.

Five days later, the Danes faced a do-or-die clash with Holland. Win and they could look to progress, lose and it was time to forget buying any postcards as they'd be home before they arrived. This time, Thomas played in place of friend Stig Tøfting, who had started against the French. Johansson realised that Thomas had to play as he was the one player they had who could conjure a split-second of brilliance out of nothing. At the top level, being organised and working hard only gets you so far. You need talented individuals to produce game-changing moments. At this point, very few football observers outside of Denmark and Germany knew who Thomas was, as coverage of the Bundesliga had yet to be beamed outside of Germany on any real scale. But he bossed the first half. He was more dynamic and easily the match of his better-known counterparts: Juventus playmaker Edgar Davids — known as the Pitbull — Phillip Cocu of Barcelona and Marc Overmars, who was at Arsenal.

It was goalless at half-time but it should have been 1-0 to Denmark. Thomas received the ball outside the penalty box, pushed it out from under his feet and fooled Dutch keeper Edwin van der Sar — one of the best stoppers of the modern era — by clipping a gorgeous, delicate chip that sailed over his hulking 6ft 5in frame, only to come crashing back off the crossbar.

Granted, it was only one effort but still it proved that on the biggest stage, with pressure on his underdog team and facing opponents with far greater reputations, Thomas was able to remain cool and calm. He could show that flash of flair and produce a telling moment of individual play. But it's a team game and the Dutch kept going, eventually winning 3-0, all their goals coming in a quickfire 20-minute period.

The Danes were out, with the Czech match now meaningless apart from avoiding being bagelled — losing every game. Fearful Johansson didn't want another pasting, so went cautious with his team selection. He swapped the more defensive, but less skilled Tøfting back in for Thomas. He was clearly worried that the adventurous youngster wouldn't have just sat back and settled for a draw to save face, and he was right. Thomas wouldn't have done that in a month of Sundays. In the event, Denmark went down 2-0, with Thomas seeing out his first international tournament rooted to the bench.

The Danes left with the worst record in the competition, but Thomas had impressed. He'd proved against arguably the two best nations in Europe that he was at a far higher level than it appeared on paper.

His performances hadn't escaped the watching eyes of the wily veteran Scottish management duo of Walter Smith and Archie Knox. They'd earned a massive reputation by leading Glasgow giants Rangers to nine league titles in a row. During that spell, they convinced big names to come to the relative backwater of Scottish football, including Brian Laudrup, who snubbed Barcelona, Oleg Salenko, who scored five goals in a single game at the 1994 World Cup, and French hard man Basile Boli.

After leaving Rangers, they'd moved to England to take over at Everton in 1998. Walter was the boss and Archie was his trusted lieutenant, a job he'd previously done for Sir Alex Ferguson at Manchester United and Aberdeen. Between them, they'd seen and done everything in the game, including unlocking one of the game's most complex characters in Paul Gascoigne. They had brought Gazza home to Britain from his Italian odyssey with Lazio in Rome and built a team around him at Rangers. The mercurial Geordie repaid them with the most consistent spell of his career. They were able to get the best out of him and get inside his head, unlike so many other managers. After they left Rangers, they brought Gazza with them to Everton and he was still in the squad that Thomas joined. After signing his contract, Thomas opted to select number 16 for himself, which was to stay with him for almost all of the remainder of his club career.

Walter and Archie had spent almost 40 years in management, handling players of all abilities and backgrounds.

But their squad then at Everton was challenging to say the least. As well as Gazza, it included Scottish beanpole striker Duncan Ferguson, who'd been jailed and become famous for 'detaining' a burglar he awoke to find in his own house, before the police arrived. Even with his experience, Archie couldn't believe how off-the-wall Thomas was. He said, 'We'd seen him in an international game and we thought, he's quite a useful player, a strong powerful lad and all the rest of it. So we made enquires and he ended up at Everton. But God almighty, he was some boy, Thomas. A livewire wouldn't cover it. He was a total one-off, you wouldn't believe some of the antics he got up to.'

Everton are a club with a rich history. Since 1892, they have played at Goodison Park, which is located to the north of Liverpool's city centre and was the first purpose-built football stadium in England. Thomas joined for £2.5 million in the summer of 2000, at a time when the Toffees had an experienced group. It included strapping Portuguese full-back Abel Xavier, Scottish centre-half Richard Gough and powerful forward Kevin Campbell. The skipper was defensive warhorse Dave Watson, who was entering his final season with Everton after joining in 1986.

There was also a decent amount of talent coming through from the youth team, players like Tony Hibbert, Kevin McLeod and Nick Chadwick. It was a well-honed unit of mixed ages, marshalled along by other experienced pros like David Weir, Steve Watson and Niclas Alexandersson. But nothing could have prepared them for this Danish enigma, who wasn't going to change anything about his approach, no matter who his new team-mates were.

Archie said, 'He just got into scrapes left, right and centre. That's the way he was but he was a powerful player. He always had plenty to say, he'd challenge everything even in training, but Thomas always insisted that he was in the right. There was never a chance of him backing down. He was that determined, to him he was *always* in the right. But he had more good about him than he had bad, there's no doubt about that.'

The team got off to a poor start, going down 2-0 away to Leeds. Thomas did not appear due to lack of fitness but he was brought in for the first home game against Charlton Athletic in what must have been the most colourful midfield partnership of all time. He lined up next to Gazza, who was supposed to be the sensible one and make sure they kept their shape and discipline. How that was supposed to work was anyone's guess but the canny Scottish duo Smith and Knox somehow managed it as the team won 3-0. Thomas kept his place in the starting 11 for the Toffees (Everton's nickname comes from Ye Ancient Everton Toffee House, which used to be close to their stadium) and got his first goal in his third appearance during a 2-2 draw with Derby. This time, it was just Thomas in midfield as Gazza was benched.

As well as always acting up and having a laugh in training, Archie was fascinated by how Thomas interacted with Gitte. She'd also left Hamburg and joined Everton's ladies' team. After he'd done his work for the day, Thomas and Gitte would do extra training and play against each other. Archie could barely believe his eyes at what one of the strongest and most powerful players in the English Premier League, known for its high degree of physicality, was up to. Archie was shocked as he saw Thomas flying into tackles and using his body as if he was in the middle of a full-blooded match. Instead, it was with his own childhood sweetheart in an indoor hall. Archie recalled, 'She played for the ladies' team and they used to go in the gym and play one v ones. But he'd batter the ball at her as if he was playing against a man. It was in the big indoor gym at Bellefield [Everton's training ground]. They'd play for ages in there, the two of them going at it.'

As things progressed, Walter and Archie both started to detect an issue that others before had encountered. Once Thomas gets an idea in his head, he's off. They realised he wouldn't stick to a position but, unlike the other managers who tried to force him to be something he wasn't, they worked with him. Archie said: 'Everybody would say, what position are you going to play him? Because he had that bit about him, where he could do things, he could deliver a pass but he wouldn't maintain that position. The ball was the attraction to him. He'd wander about the pitch looking to be on the ball. We tried him in every position, wing-back, midfield, off the front and he did well — he was a handful all right.'

When Everton welcomed the mighty Manchester United, who were at the peak of their powers after winning the Champions League as part of a historic treble (including the Premier League and FA Cup), Smith and Knox formulated a plan to get the best out of Thomas. They put five men across midfield and allowed Thomas to roam about wherever he wanted, giving him licence to get on the ball. He scored but Everton still lost 3-1.

As the season wore on, Smith and Knox realised that no matter what they said to Thomas, he was a spirit that couldn't be tamed. Archie feels Thomas did listen to tactical instructions but explained it was as if the player then subconsciously decided to ignore them. Archie said: 'He would be listening to you, but it was a case of in one ear and out the other ear. You had to say to him, "Just you go create havoc wherever you can, Thomas. Either it's for us or against us."'

Thomas's inclusion in different positions in an attempt to unlock his true potential was a metaphor for the team and reflected their overall performances — inconsistent. A great away win against Newcastle in October was tempered by losing to city rivals Liverpool, followed by a 1-0 reverse against Aston Villa. The patchy form wasn't a huge surprise as Walter and Archie had sold players for £20 million but only spent £13 million on new blood. In such a competitive league, downsizing made it nigh on impossible to have sustained on-field success. The team slipped towards the relegation zone but their experienced management duo steadied the ship, as Everton beat West Ham away then got three points against Manchester City at home before losing three on the bounce. They rebounded with a valuable win against Bradford, which saw them finish in 16th position. Manchester City (look at them now), Coventry City and Bradford City all dropped through the trapdoor out of the Premier League.

Thomas finished the season, with a new name. He'd been christened 'Mad Dog' by the Everton fans, who adopted him as a cult hero — just as supporters had in Hamburg. The English fans loved his style of steaming about the pitch and going in full force on opponents, regardless of the consequences. It was as if they were watching a guy in the local park getting the chance to play one game as a superstar pro. The irony is, Thomas played every single match like that, and it's why he was so popular.

He was a mainstay in the starting 11, with Gazza and others being sacrificed to accommodate him as the months wore on, and Thomas's strength and power made him a natural fit for the demanding league. He acquitted himself with aplomb in a struggling team and considering the Premier League's team of the year included top performers like Roy Keane, Patrick Vieira, Harry Kewell, David Beckham and Andy Cole, that was no mean feat.

He also ended his first year in Liverpool with an accent that was to add to his oddness. He developed an unusual

Scouse/Danish hybrid, but it was more the habit he picked up of calling everyone 'lad'. It became his calling card and if you hear anyone tell a Thomas Gravesen story, when they recount what he said, Thomas will end most sentences with his ubiquitous 'lad'.

Oh, and he also didn't go by Thomas any longer — now he'd been adopted by Everton's faithful and was known more fondly as Tommy.

Chapter 7
Mike Tyson's Idol

OVER the summer, Everton's financial position didn't improve and some players had to be moved on. Out went one of their crown jewels, young left-back Michael Ball, who had made his debut for England a few months earlier. He went to Glasgow Rangers for £6.5 million. Arsène Wenger moved for the striker he'd billed as 'the fox in the box', Francis Jeffers, bringing an initial £8 million into the coffers. Gazza had been away in Arizona at a rehab clinic getting treatment for alcohol addiction. The only new blood was youngster Leon Osman, who had graduated from the youth team, and Canadian goalscorer Tomasz Radzinski, for £4.5 million, who arrived from Belgian side Anderlecht.

But the odds were stacked against Everton as other clubs were splashing out on a far grander scale. Manchester United signed Juan Sebastián Verón for £28.1 million, a

British record at the time, and Dutch goal-getter Ruud van Nistelrooy for £19 million. Chelsea got French World Cup winner Emmanuel Petit for £7.5 million from Barcelona. Liverpool locked down prodigy Michael Owen on a new £70,000-a-week deal. Tottenham landed German wing-back Christian Ziege and defender Dean Richards for a combined £12.1 million.

Also part of that Everton squad was a precocious Wayne Rooney. While he had yet to make his first-team debut, everyone at the club knew he was destined for great things. He would announce himself the following season with his iconic 30-yard goal against Arsenal but he was already making waves. Observers were staggered by his ability and the hype had become so great that the media began to take a keen interest in the teenage prodigy.

Full-back Tony Hibbert, who spent his whole career at Everton and made over 300 appearances, saw Rooney's career first hand at all stages. Tony admitted, 'People will think Wayne Rooney was the most talented I've played with — and he could pull a volley out of nothing and put it in the top corner from 35 yards, like he did against Arsenal. But ability-wise, Thomas Gravesen was the best. For passing and skills, he was different class.'

This from a low-key individual who, despite being regularly mentioned on TV football shows and in sports newspaper coverage for over a decade, could walk down most streets in Britain unrecognised. For someone like

Hibbert to pop up and say that is a signal he means it. It's not a ploy to garner column inches.

The Toffees began the 2001/02 season brightly with a 2-1 win away at Charlton. Thomas set up the winner by swinging in a delightful corner that David Weir fired home with his right foot. They followed it with a 2-0 victory over Middlesbrough but the squad's inconsistency surfaced again when they went down 4-1 to Manchester United the following weekend — both without Thomas.

Walter and Archie restored Thomas to the starting 11 for the first Merseyside derby as Everton took an early lead thanks to Kevin Campbell, but then Steven Gerrard, Michael Owen and new recruit John Arne Riise scored to take the three points back to Anfield. No one knew what was coming next. Everton lost to Blackburn but rebounded with a 5-0 thumping of West Ham, with Thomas running 40 yards with the ball before unleashing a bullet that flew past helpless keeper Shaka Hislop.

Club captain David Weir had been watching the new midfielder closely and was fascinated by Thomas. Weir said, 'He was very different. He could be very morose and very cold, and then on other occasions he was larger than life and full of fun. You never really knew what mood he was going to be in. It seemed to be from one extreme to the other. He was a loose cannon and physically he was so, so strong. If there was something he didn't want to do, he just wouldn't do it. In training when he gave the ball away, we'd say "Thomas you gave that ball away, so you have to go in the middle." He'd just look at you and say: "No, I'm not going in," and he just wouldn't. If he was in that mood, he was the most stubborn man ever and if he thought he was right, he just refused to do something he felt was wrong. But he was super-talented and a match-winner.'

David's analysis proved spot on as Thomas was to deliver an all-round devastating 90 minutes that Cristiano Ronaldo has since made his trademark during his glittering career. Denmark were now managed by ex-Ajax boss Morten Olsen, who'd taken the reins after their tepid Euro 2000 appearance, where the team were caught between a rock and a hard place about how to set up tactically. One of the first things he did was make Thomas a key player. He was nailed on as a starter and Olsen placed all his confidence in Mad Dog's ability. The rest of the team would be built around him. Morten Wieghorst was one who noticed the change in approach to Thomas in the Danish training camps from frustration to compassion. 'Mr Olsen knew him very well and when Thomas started to walk off the line, Mr Olsen would call him back straight away and ask him to focus. For whatever reason, I don't know, Thomas's mind would wander even though he was deadly serious about his football. He could start doing his own thing and he needed reminding.'

Olsen realised that Thomas needed someone to watch his back, plug holes and be defensively switched on, as once he saw the ball, he would sprint off and forget his responsibility to keep the back door shut. Stig Tøfting, a hard man who ironically had joined HSV after Thomas left, was handed the role of his on-field minder. The pair gelled well, on and off the pitch. The new approach worked wonders, things clicked into place and the players were clearly more comfortable as they went through their ten-game qualifying campaign for the 2002 World Cup unbeaten. They won six, drew four and topped their group ahead of the Czech Republic, Bulgaria, Northern Ireland and Malta, scoring 22 goals and conceding only six. It was quite a turnaround from Euro 2000, where they'd been the whipping boys. It was imperious stuff and for the final game of the qualifying stage at Copenhagen's Parken Stadium in October 2001, 41,769 fans packed inside for the visit of Iceland. It became a match of legend, with Danes still reminiscing about the night their number seven served up an irresistible performance as they triumphed 6-0.

Thomas set up the second goal. After a deep cross went way past the back post, he scurried to reach it and with an almighty jump, powered an inch-perfect header back across for penalty box king Ebbe Sand to tap in. Iceland then tried to play out from the back when a prowling Thomas stripped the defender with his right foot and carried the ball into the penalty box at speed before deftly chipping the keeper with his left foot. Thomas then tore the roof off when Tøfting tapped a free kick to him 40 yards out in the middle of the pitch. He ran up and gave the ball such an almighty lashing that it flew into the top corner like a missile. Power, skill, left foot, right foot, using his head, game intelligence, sprinting all over the pitch, intercepting passes — Thomas showed everything. It really was the type of display that Portugal's Ronaldo was later to master and the reason he was anointed the world's best player.

That night, Thomas was the king of Denmark as supporters in the stadium went berserk and millions of others toasted his name in their living rooms and pubs across the country. They were heading to the World Cup with one of the world's most talented players in their ranks. What really tickled them pink was the fact that not only was Thomas showing his skills, he was charging about the pitch, flying into tackles and closing people down. The veins were popping out of Thomas's neck that night. It was the match of his life and he had inspired his nation. Very few athletes manage to time their best performances and deliver when it matters most. It's why the British athletes who won six golds at London's Olympics in 2012 and saw the day dubbed 'Super Saturday', will live on in the memory long after they've passed away.

But it wasn't only the nation of Denmark that he had captivated that night. Up in the stands was Iron Mike Tyson, who was in Copenhagen for his upcoming heavyweight bout against Dane Brian Nielsen, which was to be held at the same stadium. Tyson had been given tickets to come to the match and sample the atmosphere. While it was partly a promotional junket, he was genuinely transfixed by Thomas. The one moment that really got Tyson's attention was when Thomas battled it out in his trademark combative style with three Iceland players. They all ended up on their backsides and Thomas breezed away with the ball.

Word came down to the dressing room after the final whistle that the so-called Baddest Man on the Planet saw a kindred spirit and respected Thomas's toughness. Tyson asked if it would be possible to have the honour of getting his number seven shirt.

Here was one of the world's most famous athletes and sportsmen of any era, who'd earned a reported $700 million, asking if he could get Thomas's shirt as a souvenir. Thomas said, 'Apparently, he was a bit impressed with the way I played. I'd like to think it was down to the two goals I scored but I was told that what he really liked was my attitude to the game, and the way I looked after myself. But it still came as a massive surprise afterwards when he said he wanted my shirt. It gave me a real lift to think that the great Mike Tyson wanted my jersey as a souvenir.'

For the rest of his time in Copenhagen, Tyson walked around proudly in Thomas's number seven top in tribute to his new hero. Still, Thomas didn't get too sentimental. He publicly predicted that Nielsen would win – but unlike his magical display against Iceland, he got his boxing analysis horribly wrong. Tyson won inside seven rounds to set up a blockbuster bout against Lennox Lewis.

Thomas touched down back in Liverpool with a spring in his step. His first game since his spellbinding performance against Iceland was against Aston Villa. An interesting subplot was that Thomas's international team-mate Peter Schmeichel was in goal for the visitors. Everton raced into a 1-0 lead thanks to Steve Watson and not long after were awarded a free kick on the edge of the penalty box. Thomas and Schmeichel eyed each other like a pair of Texan gunslingers. Both were well aware of their respective strengths and weaknesses after many Danish training camps together. Scot Gemmill touched the ball to the side, just like Tøfting had done weeks before, and Thomas ripped his boot through it. It went under the defensive wall and into the lower left corner of the net. Schmeichel only dived once it had flown past him. Schmeichel nearly had the last laugh as he went up for a corner and scored to ensure a nervy end to the game, but the Toffees clung on to win 3-2.

Walter and Archie desperately needed to bolster the team's attacking options and handed a deal to ex-Manchester United winger Jesper Blomqvist, who had not played for two years due to injury. At times Thomas, thanks to his all-round ability, had even been pressed into playing as an emergency striker. This lack of resources was probably the biggest factor in Everton's helter-skelter form. They lost to Newcastle and drew with Bolton after defender Alan Stubbs scored a free kick following Thomas's touch to him, which was still rising as it hit the back of the net.

The team lost to Chelsea and Leicester before Southampton came to Goodison. Radzinski gave them the lead and it turned into an old-fashioned end-to-end scrap. Thomas was put through on goal and instead of blasting it, tried to delicately dink it but a defender cleared it off the line. Getting a second bite at the cherry, it bounced back to him and he again tried a cheeky flick, but it still didn't come off. The Sky Sports cameras flashed to Walter Smith, who was apoplectic in the dugout. He wanted Thomas to smash it home and secure the win Everton badly needed. Thomas was never one to do the easy thing or play it safe; that's how he was wired.

Co-commentator Andy Gray told the watching millions gripped by the pulsating match, 'You don't often see Walter Smith show that kind of reaction. Put your foot through it, that for me is just a waste.' A few minutes later Thomas left the same pundit silent as, in the middle of a war zone, he pulled off a 360 spin, like a ballerina at the Bolshoi, beat one man, then went past another two. He was up for it that night. Gray had no option but to sing Thomas's praises minutes later when he swung over what he described as 'a magnificent cross' for Mark Pembridge to bundle the ball home and seal a 2-0 win. He did it his way, but Thomas got the team there in the end.

Soon afterwards, Thomas sparked off what was the beginning of his cult relationship with the Everton fans. During a home match against Derby County just before

Christmas, Thomas was involved in a nasty clash of heads with Darryl Powell. They both fell to the ground with blood pouring from deep gashes as the nearest player to the incident, Steve Watson, turned away in horror. As Thomas was being stretched off to hospital barely semi-conscious, the crowd sang his name and he began fist pumping wildly, even though he was constrained by a neck brace.

After shaking off his injury, Thomas came back but, like the previous season, Everton couldn't find any consistency. Fulham beat them then they won at Derby before heading to the North East to face Sunderland. Up to this point, Thomas had managed to keep a lid on his temper. Smith and Knox were able to keep him focused and he was flying at international level. Thomas had also begun to earn the respect of fans across England.

For the next match, at Sunderland's Stadium of Light, there was pressure on Everton to get a win as they were struggling close to the bottom of the table. Thomas was wound up and exploded into life by hacking down Julio Arca after only three minutes. Referee Barry Knight flashed a yellow card, the earliest booking of that entire season. The warning just made Thomas angrier. He continued to rampage about and smashed into Arca again. The referee ran over to admonish Thomas and would have been well within his rights to brandish a red card. But Walter and Archie knew that it was only a matter of time, so Thomas was substituted after 27 minutes. It was a public embarrassment for a top player but the team had to come first. Even with that, they still lost.

Thomas didn't even last that long in the next match against Manchester United. After a tangle with Gary Neville, he limped off just eight minutes into the first half. Everton went down 2-0 and then lost 3-0 to Charlton to round off 2001. It was a dark, depressing end to the year, with the pressure increasing on everyone at the club.

He didn't know it then but Thomas would only play another 77 minutes for Walter and Archie. He only recovered enough to come on as a half-time substitute against Liverpool at Anfield in late February, a match that ended in a 1-1 draw. Nicolas Anelka levelled after Everton's Radzinski opened the scoring. Next were cameos against Leeds United and West Ham.

Sadly, while Thomas had been on the treatment table, the team's form went awry, beginning with a loss to Middlesbrough then revenge over Sunderland with a 1-0 home win. But it was a frustrating one-step-forward, two-steps-backwards routine. Walter and Archie were fighting with one hand tied behind their backs, as without any serious financial clout it was impossible to move up the league and compete.

One of their worst moments was when the Everton board sanctioned the transfer of Abel Xavier to city rivals Liverpool. He was only the fourth player to cross the divide in that direction and it summed up the situation: Everton were willing to sell anyone if the price was right. Walter and Archie were sacked in March 2002 as the panicked board of directors feared that relegation could become a reality. Dropping out the league would have meant a huge loss of TV revenue and also a fall in the value of the players, who would be looked on as failures by some in the game. Ironically, it was one of their last acts in charge at Goodison that was to propel Thomas to global stardom.

They signed Lee Carsley, a workmanlike defensive midfielder, from Coventry City. He had no glamour and was not the type of player to excite fans but he was functional. A bit like getting a new handbrake on your Ferrari. Carsley was to have a pivotal influence on Thomas, the perfect Robin to his Batman, although neither knew it at the time. Nor did new boss David Moyes, who was appointed as Everton's new manager after some sterling work in the lower leagues with Preston North End.

Thomas was about to embark on a dizzying ascent that would turn him into a Galáctico, but in his erratic world it was about to get off to the worst possible start.

Chapter 8

The Green Nissan Micra

MOYES had only been appointed 48 hours ahead of the next home game against Fulham, who at the time played silky football under the command of their flamboyant French coach Jean Tigana. Spurred on by their passionate supporters, Everton won a penalty and took the lead inside 60 seconds thanks to David Unsworth, who despite being a rugged defender scored 22 spot kicks in his career. Duncan Ferguson doubled the lead and they were on easy street.

Then entered Thomas, who'd already got himself booked after a tackle on jet-heeled winger Luís Boa Morte. Without his old management team on the sidelines to calm him down, and driven by an earnest schoolboy mentality that meant he desperately wanted to impress his new manager,

Thomas careered about the pitch before recklessly launching into midfield opponent John Collins. The referee had no option but to flash a red card. So with 28 minutes on the clock, Everton were down to ten men and having to hold on grimly for a much-needed win. They managed it but Fulham made them sweat after pulling a goal back in the second half. It was a foolish move by Thomas. He'd let his emotions overcome him almost to the detriment of the team, and under the watchful eye of a new manager.

Nevertheless, Moyes could clearly see Thomas's ability in training and played him in the next game, as his suspension was due to kick in at a later date. Going from villain to hero in a single moment, Thomas showed how at times of chaos and frenetic action, he could be the coolest guy on the pitch. The ball broke to him on the edge of Derby's box and he fooled the defenders by playing a quick, first-time ball to the onrushing Unsworth, who opened the scoring to set up a 4-3 away victory for Everton. It was typical Thomas. As everyone had started to tighten up with nerves, he kept playing the same way he had since his days in the park with his mates in Vejle. With a ball at his feet, everything made sense.

The ship had been steadied somewhat and Moyes managed to grind out the results. In the end, Everton were safe by a fair margin, finishing in 15th, seven points above the dreaded relegation zone, and much to the acclaim of their fans, who couldn't countenance dropping down into the lower leagues. The squad were about to start their summer break but Thomas's team-mates had begun to notice an odd habit. Thomas had spent the winter driving a well-used Nissan Micra, a small starter car. There was nothing wrong with it as a means of transport but it was not the sort of motor that other well-paid professional footballers were driving — and it stood out in the Everton players' car park.

David Weir, for one, was puzzled by it. Not that one of his team-mates had opted for a cheap, simple car, but that he would only drive it in cold, rainy weather. Once the sun came out, Thomas would show up in a series of flash sports cars or jeeps. David said, 'I remember at one stage he was driving that Micra and in the summer he'd have three or four top-of-the-range cars that cost £100,000 and he'd rotate them. But it would just be this one basic car in the winter. That sums him up and that's how Thomas was. He'd say, "Why would I drive nice cars in the bad weather?" You couldn't predict Thomas.' Fellow team-mate Kevin Campbell also struggled to take it in, adding, 'He [Thomas] bought himself these lovely cars. He bought an F50 pick-up truck and he had a Porsche and another car. Then months later, I came in and there's a banged-up Nissan Micra in the car park. I asked the kitman, "Whose is that?" He said, "Thomas Gravesen has sold all his cars and that's his car." For six months, Thomas Gravesen was rolling around Liverpool in a green Nissan Micra. He was mad as a box of frogs.' Despite a patchy second half of the season for Everton, Thomas had remained a key part of the Danish set-up and was on the plane to South Korea and Japan that summer. It was to be his first — and only — World Cup. In a move that reflected his importance to the squad, he was given the number seven shirt. His good friend Stig Tøfting was also in the 23-man party and his role was key in allowing Thomas to roam. Tøfting would hold his position and do the defensive work. They were two kindred spirits who liked to have a laugh off the pitch, but they also worked very effectively in tandem on it. But together, they got Denmark's campaign off to a disastrous start.

At the pre-tournament training camp, Thomas and Tøfting, both strong, burly men, ambushed slightly built winger Jesper Grønkjær. They put ice cubes down his shorts, then Thomas and Tøfting took it in turns to pin him down and spray his face with water bottles from a matter of inches. Their team-mate, who was playing for Chelsea at the time, didn't find it funny and lashed out at Tøfting, who fought back and grabbed Grønkjær around the throat as Thomas waded in.

Even worse, the scuffle played out in front of the Danish press, who were there to cover the team's World Cup build-up. The management were naturally not pleased and an official snapped: 'These players need a kindergarten teacher to sort them out.' The whole incident was splashed on the front pages of newspapers and dominated the agenda back home, putting both Thomas and Tøfting firmly in the doghouse.

Danish football journalist Johan Lyngholm-Bjerge said: 'It was only for fun but the media wrote about a big fight. All the players thought it was ridiculous and the national coach was angry that they made it such a big deal. Then big news agencies like Reuters took the story on, too, so it went worldwide about this clash in the Danish World Cup squad.'

Thomas took it personally and felt under attack, and it was then that he started cutting back on interviews — not that he'd ever been that prolific. But he was beginning to pull the shutters down as the media-saturated modern world clashed with his maverick ways. Ironically, the incident only served to fuel interest in Thomas's madcap lifestyle and sparkling skills. 'For alm ost a decade, he was one of the most interesting sports personalities in Denmark,' Lyngholm-Bjerge recalled. 'He was very much in the media. He wasn't the boring footballer who spoke in clichés like "it's only about the next game" and that sort of stuff. When he was playing, it was with a big smile, making jokes, and he was a fantastic footballer to watch with great technique, always with full power in the tackles. That's what the fans loved.'

Eventually, things were patched up and the Danes headed east to take their place in Group A. Once again, they'd been handed a tough draw and most tipsters predicted they'd soon be going home in quick fashion. In their group were defending champions France, Uruguay and Senegal.

Their opening match was in the Munsu Stadium in the Korean city of Ulsan. The venue had been purpose-built for the competition. Thomas was in the centre of midfield with partner Tøfting beside him. Some neutrals struggled to tell them apart as they both had shaven heads and similarly powerful builds. From a distance, it was easy to confuse them. Alongside them in the starting 11 was Grønkjær, their embarrassing incident now put to bed.

Uruguay were the opposition and had some top players in their side. Captain Paolo Montero was a no-nonsense defender at Juventus and striker Alvaro Recoba was a star at Inter Milan. In the last minute of the first half, Thomas started a move that led to a cross being sent into the penalty box for Jon Dahl Tomasson to fire the Danes ahead. Dario Rodriguez equalised for the South Americans in the second half but with seven minutes left on the clock, Tomasson snatched a winner.

Denmark were off to a dream start. The public back home were in raptures and the team were buzzing as winning the opening match in any tournament allows momentum to build.

The following day, though, they were rocked by another media scandal. It had been an open secret in the Danish football world that when Tøfting was 13, his father had killed his mother before committing suicide. But it was now being publicised by *SE og HØR* (See and Hear) magazine and put Tøfting in a difficult position. Everyone now knew his family's history, including his own children, who were forced to discover it in a very crass, public way. The entire squad felt under attack on Tøfting's behalf, with Thomas feeling it more than most. Here was his friend's private anguish being exposed to the wider world. The storm only hardened Thomas's attitude towards granting interviews and his general distaste for media interest. Captain Jan Heintze read out a statement on behalf of the squad that said, 'We are also upset about the fact that the article deprives Stig Tøfting and his wife, Bettina, the chance to inform their children, aged seven, eight and 12, about the destiny of their biological grandparents and the relations within the family in their own words. We are, however, determined that this story should not interfere in any negative way in our ambitions and objectives for this World Cup and are therefore hoping for the understanding of the media that we will not accept any questions on this issue.'

It's not uncommon for adversity to draw people together and it has happened many times in football. The media onslaught over the previous few weeks did just that for the Danes. They went into their second game with Senegal fighting against the establishment and with fire in their bellies — and they needed it. The West Africans had a raft of players like El Hadji Diouf, Papa Bouba Diop, Salif Diao and Henri Camara, who'd made their names at big European clubs. They'd already proved their mettle by shocking France with a 1-0 win in their opening game. Both teams were riding high and the 43,500 fans packed into the Daegu Stadium were in for a pulsating match. Denmark, with Thomas and

Tøfting dovetailing like Ginger Rogers and Fred Astaire, took the lead thanks to a penalty from that man again, Tomasson. Diao levelled the scores and that's how it ended. While a win would obviously have better suited both teams, a point apiece kept them both well in the hunt to qualify as Uruguay and France played out a dull 0-0 draw.

The Danes had a hell of a task in their final group game. Although they were in pole position, they were still battling to secure one of the top two places. Wounded after a poor start, the French were bound to be dangerous opponents. Their team sheet had arguably their greatest ever player in Zinedine Zidane and huge talents like Vieira, Thuram and Desailly were all still around. Some new blood had also been added in the shape of defensive midfield visionary Claude Makélélé and prolific forward Djibril Cissé. The French were facing a barrage of criticism back home, with their fans outraged that such a talented squad could deliver such lukewarm performances. For the Danes, Morten Olsen stuck with his usual system of Thomas and Tøfting together in the middle of the park.

With everything on the line and facing a midfield of the highest quality, Thomas rose to the occasion just like he'd done many times before. When the stakes were high and skill was needed to compete, that's when Thomas showed his mettle. Olsen understood him, too, so was able to keep him focused and primed to control the game. That's exactly what he did. Thomas bossed Zidane and the rest of them off the pitch. There was only one sheriff in Incheon that afternoon and it was Denmark's number seven.

With 22 minutes on the clock, Thomas challenged Zidane and the ball broke to Tøfting on the right-hand side of the pitch, near France's penalty box. He clipped a ball to the back post towards Dennis Rommedahl, who fired it past Fabien Barthez. France couldn't get near Thomas, who was on the biggest stage of all with a manager who believed in him. He was showing what everyone in Vejle knew — that Thomas was world class. Then, in the second half, he got the ball near the halfway line and delivered a pinpoint pass that split France's famed defence apart. The ball travelled 35 yards but was so beautifully timed that Grønkjær didn't have to break stride to knock over a simple cross. Tomasson was there waiting to tap it in. It was sheer class from Thomas.

Shell-shocked France were heading for the baggage carousel at Charles de Gaulle and Denmark had won the group with seven points against all the odds — thanks in no small part to their inspirational maverick midfielder. There's a wonderful picture on FIFA's website of Thomas and Zidane competing. Thomas has his teeth clenched, wide eyes fixed on the ball, looking dynamic and full of purpose. Zidane looks weary, tired and visibly lacking the belief that he'd win the duel. He didn't. Thomas won the battle — and this particular war too.

In the round of 16, England were next up for the Danes. It was the ideal game for Thomas to shine as he faced most of the players regularly with Everton. The midfield line-up for the Three Lions that night was David Beckham, Paul Scholes, Nicky Butt and Trevor Sinclair. It was the ideal contest for Thomas to revel in, he played against them on a weekly basis so knew what sort of tempo and intensity to expect.

But that familiarity proved his downfall. Without the edge he'd had against France, when it was do or die, he didn't perform. His wayward display cost the team dearly and he was at fault for England's second goal. After a cross from the left by Sinclair, Butt helped it on for Michael Owen to score, with Thomas arriving a split second too late to prevent the pass. If he'd stayed in position and kept his focus on doing the simple things, maybe he'd have stopped that goal. In the end, England won 3-0 and marched on to face Brazil.

The Danes were out but left with their heads held high. They'd made up for their Euro 2000 disaster and proved they could play slick, attacking football. Thomas left the World Cup, too, with his reputation bolstered. He'd shown moments of true class in all of the games, confounding those who still thought he was just a bull in a china shop who dived into tackles. Ultimately, it was his character and ego that led to the worst elements of his game resurfacing. On the biggest stage against the world's best players, there was no room for error.

Thomas would have to learn a hard lesson from the World Cup: that he had to stay dialled in for every single second at the highest level. He had to focus more. But the great thing for football fans far and wide was the penny had dropped and he was about to shift up a gear into overdrive.

Chapter 9

Bending it Better than Beckham

THOMAS returned to Liverpool with a spring in his step. He'd been to the pinnacle and done the business. Moyes was also set to start his first full season in charge of Everton and a teenage Wayne Rooney had been promoted to the first team. The manager couldn't hold him back any longer as he had the physical attributes of a fully grown man and had to be unleashed. But within the squad Thomas was still seen as the special one, the guy they could rely on to deliver the unexpected.

Central defender Alan Stubbs explained how the senior pros had made it clear to Thomas that there was a line he couldn't cross. 'We had some strong characters and personalities,' Stubbs said. 'Thomas would sometimes try and do things but quite quickly he was told in no uncertain terms it wasn't acceptable. At times, whether he liked it or not and after cooling down, he'd be very apologetic if he was having a tantrum. He would get frustrated, maybe kick some balls away and then after five or ten minutes, he would come across and say, "I'm sorry, I was out of order." After a while, we got used to it.'

With the senior players starting to get a grip on Thomas, they knew it was only a matter of time before he won over any remaining doubters. Stubbs added, 'We all knew what Thomas's ability was. Thomas could have been as good as Thomas wanted to be, he was very talented.'

Moyes engendered a strong spirit and began season 2002/03 with largely the same squad, bar Rooney, Nigerian defender Joseph Yobo and Chinese midfielder Li Tie.

They started with a 2-2 draw at Tottenham but even with Rooney, there was now an appreciation from the manager and players about how Thomas was going to be used. Gone were the days of trying to force him into a position that he wouldn't stick to. They had seen the potential of their most potent weapon at the World Cup and knew how to harness it. Stubbs said, 'Thomas had a way where he saw himself playing in a team and when Thomas felt he was being restricted or tied down, that's when he found it difficult to express himself. Thomas wanted to go on the pitch and play with freedom. Sometimes from Thomas's point of view, that probably wasn't the case. Sometimes it was frustrating but he would produce real moments of quality where if you hadn't allowed him that freedom, he wouldn't have produced those moments. For me, it was getting that right balance of when he needed to be disciplined and when he needed to be able to express himself, and play how Thomas wanted to play. With what we had, Thomas was the one who was a little bit different. We had some similar hard-working players but Thomas was the one who could produce moments of real quality. As a result of that, we knew Thomas was different and we had to allow him to be able to do that.'

The plan worked and Everton found much more consistency than their previous turgid seasons. They won away at Sunderland, drew with Birmingham and a few weeks later welcomed Middlesbrough to Goodison. They went 1-0 down before Kevin Campbell equalised then sealed the win after Thomas had whipped in a vicious corner that targeted Campbell's head like a laser beam. This was precisely the type of game Everton would have lost or drawn in previous years but now, with a new solidity, they showed grit and determination, with Thomas sprinkling his stardust on top.

A huge factor in the unlocking of Thomas was the influence of Lee Carsley. He'd become what Tøfting was for Thomas in the Danish team. Ironically, all three of them were bald, stocky and hard for many watching to tell apart except by their mothers. Carsley picked up the slack for Thomas. He wasn't blessed with anything like his midfield partner's natural talent or skill, but he was a hard worker who'd run his socks off. He'd do all the hard yards as Thomas went rampaging about the pitch.

It was no coincidence with this type of player next to him that Thomas excelled. He didn't have to feel boxed in and could let his natural game flow. He could play without having to make compromises. As a result, Everton reaped the rewards as Thomas ran games even at the time when he was seriously outgunned. Everton were still relative paupers compared to the big spenders.

That season saw some mega deals, such as Manchester United spending £30 million on Leeds defender Rio Ferdinand and their arch rivals City landing Paris Saint-Germain striker Nicolas Anelka for £13 million. In addition, young Italian forward Massimo Maccarone left Empoli for Middlesbrough in exchange for £8.5 million.

Even though Thomas was consistently delivering the goods on the pitch, the squad were still in a state of shock over some of his unorthodox behaviour. As Thomas was so strong, he'd begun a favourite pastime of his, grabbing someone and locking them in a fearsome bear hug. The thing was because he had so much power, which seemed innate as he didn't go to the gym, no one could get out of it. It didn't matter how big or strong they were. There were no particular targets; Thomas would just decide someone was getting a squeeze, creep up on them and pounce. The unsuspecting victim then had to look rather stupid as they dangled with their feet off the ground, helpless, as everyone else sniggered. Once Thomas felt he'd had enough, he'd let go and dump the red-faced victim on their backside.

His random switching of cars was still in full swing, with a similar replacement for his much talked-about Nissan Micra reappearing as the bad weather set in. Alan Stubbs said, 'One day it'd be that, then the week after he was in a Porsche 911 Turbo. I'd ask him what it was all about and he'd tell me. "It's dead quick, lad, and it's great for parking in Liverpool. I can get in all the little spaces." Thomas wasn't into clothes or things like that. He was not interested. He is a guy who lived for the moment and not for next year. He was like Tom Hanks in that movie *Big*, where the guy is a young boy. That's Thomas — nothing he did would ever surprise you.'

That September, Everton travelled to the West Midlands to face Aston Villa. They were playing their usual system, with Thomas in his cherished creative role, but this time his disciplined sidekick Carsley was not alongside him. The game showed the gift and the curse of Thomas Gravesen. The centre of the pitch was so wide open that you could have driven an articulated lorry through it and Villa scored twice as Thomas went everywhere without the slightest regard for keeping the back door shut. But then he got the ball on the left wing, used his freakish strength to hold off respected pro Mark Kinsella, skipped past two more players like they were mannequins and slipped an incisive reverse pass into the feet of Radzinski to score. Shortly afterwards,

Thomas lined up a corner and with his wand of a right foot, landed it on the head of Campbell to get Everton's second. It wasn't enough as Villa snatched a winner five minutes from time, but Thomas had made his presence felt. He was an undoubted match-winner but needed someone to mind the shop when he was away on his fruitful escapades.

A few weeks later, Wayne Rooney announced himself to the world by rattling home that scorching 35-yard strike against Arsenal, who were on a 30-game unbeaten run at the time. It's one of the most watched goals ever and was the moment the teenage upstart confirmed he was going to be a global star. Thomas played a part in it, too. The ball was bouncing about in midfield and Thomas had a split second glance to see Rooney looking to get in behind the Arsenal defence. So he played an up-and-under to turn the centre-backs, Rooney brought it down perfectly and the rest is history. Some media reports credited Carsley with the pass upfield, but it was definitely Thomas. At first glance, it looked like a hopeless punt but watching carefully Thomas's intention was clear. He looked up and knew what he was doing. That goal, Rooney's emergence and Thomas's sparkling form meant it was a great year for Everton fans. They were winning more than they were losing for a change.

By November, they'd won four games in a row in the Premier League for the first time ever thanks to a 1-0 win over Charlton as Thomas used his masterful passing ability to put Radzinski through on goal. That became five at Blackburn Rovers. West Bromwich Albion were the next victims and it was now an incredible six on the bounce. The streak pushed Everton up to the dizzy heights of third spot and capped an impressive turnaround after years of scrapping away.

While Rooney was attracting a lot of attention due to his age and potential, Thomas was the brains of the team. It was him who was pulling the strings and always a starter when fit, whereas Moyes tended to play Rooney from the bench quite often as he didn't want to burn the youngster out.

The team kept picking up points as they went through the Christmas period and into spring before they welcomed new champions Manchester United in what was a massive match on Merseyside. Everton needed a win to finish in the top six and nail down a European place. They took the lead once again when Thomas whipped over a delicious ball for Campbell to head home. But goals from Ruud van Nistelrooy and David Beckham, who scored a trademark free kick, meant Everton ended the day in seventh position. They'd cruelly lost out on a place in the UEFA Cup by a single point.

It was a season that had promised so much but ended with nothing apart from a new-found respect from their fans and rivals. They'd shown they could turn the tables and go after teams, and that they were better than the last few years had shown.

It was Thomas's best campaign in English football so far as Everton squeezed out every ounce of effort. He'd played

33 league games and helped his team deliver a sparkling season. He was skilful but he also charged about like a lion, spurring on and inspiring his team-mates.

Thomas was also in great form for Denmark. Just like Rooney, Beckham shot to global acclaim after a single goal in 1996, when Golden Balls (as he was nicknamed by wife Victoria) whipped the ball over hapless Wimbledon keeper Neil Sullivan from the halfway line in a Premier League game at Selhurst Park. Beckham hoisted both arms into the air and from then on was a household name. Legendary TV commentator Martin Tyler said, 'You knew history was being made in front of your eyes, firstly because of the audacity and technical ability of the goal. It had bravado, brilliance and technique.' Well, Thomas did it too, probably even better. The difference was his attempt was overshadowed by his penis.

The Danes were in Bucharest to take on Romania in their Euro 2004 qualifying campaign. It was a tight group, with Norway and Bosnia and Herzegovina in the hunt for the top two places. Morten Olsen had the Danish lads primed to deliver in what was going to be an intimidating atmosphere inside the rowdy 55,000-capacity Stadionul National.

Claus Jensen was a clean-cut kind of guy, an elegant midfielder who at the time played for Charlton Athletic. After a training session, he was lying down having his picture taken by a photographer. Unbeknown to him, cheeky Thomas was straddling him and then squatted down, yanking up his shorts and underpants so his scrotum and penis were dangling a few centimetres from Claus' shaven head. The sight of a famous footballer exposing his genitals was big news and the image of the prank went around the world. It gave Thomas an unwanted reputation as a clown — and a bad-tempered one at that. Olsen was furious as the team's preparations had been disrupted yet again by Thomas's crazy antics. A Danish sports reporter said, 'Sometimes he's our genius, sometimes he's an idiot. The best that can be said is that it's not a secret what he keeps in his pants.'

Thomas went on to the pitch with another media storm swirling around him, but yet again it didn't bother him in the slightest as, in his eyes, he'd only been having a laugh. He never saw any harm in that sort of thing and was not fazed by the attention it drew.

During the match, he showed just why Olsen was prepared to tolerate his misdemeanours. The home team were up 2-1 in a pulsating match, when the Romanian keeper snuffed out an attack by booting the ball way downfield. It landed a few yards inside Romania's half but as he scampered back, Thomas assessed the situation in a flash and smashed the ball first time into the net. The game ended in a 5-2 win for Denmark.

Beckham's version got a lot more attention but if you compare them, Thomas's effort deserves more credit. Becks has time, the ball is rolling slowly in front of him and he runs on to it unobstructed. Thomas had no time as a Romanian player was in his face, chasing after the ball, and he hit it first time. It was an instinctive act of genius. Very few players would have been able to see the picture so fast and even fewer would have had the bottle to try something as daring. Thomas made it look effortless. As soon as he struck it, you knew it was in. It capped a few days that only Thomas was capable of manufacturing. It's just a shame that his trouser snake took all the attention away from what was a jaw-dropping goal, and the best of his career.

Chapter 10

Fun in the Sun

THOMAS maintained his sparkling form over the summer and made the difference again in Denmark's friendly against Ukraine. It was a warm-up for the next round of qualifying games for Euro 2004. The Copenhagen crowd saw Claus Jensen – who had put Willygate behind him – flight over a teasing corner and Thomas rose like an albatross to bullet it home. It was yet another display of the all-round game that Thomas had; he really could do it all. The win powered Denmark on. They beat Norway and did the same against Luxembourg, with Thomas netting again with what was described in the media as an 'unstoppable shot'.

It was all part of a superb campaign that saw the Danes top the qualifying group and book their place in Portugal with only one loss in eight games. Coupled with how they'd performed in the previous World Cup, Denmark were one of Europe's form sides. They had found their groove, with Thomas as their beating heart, although he was now without sidekick Tøfting, who'd retired from international duty.

When he returned to Everton for what would be his third season (2003/04) in the English game, it was clear Thomas felt at ease. Everton are a big club with a proud history but at the time there was a homely atmosphere without too many outrageous egos. It's clear there were parallels with Vejle for Thomas. He was part of a community and knew everyone in what was a tight-knit group. It was no coincidence that in this type of environment, he was able to thrive and deliver the goods, which would soon take him away from Everton.

Young Scottish forward James McFadden joined Everton from Motherwell that summer and was surprised by how cosy it was. He said, 'For all it was a massive club, it had a wee rundown training ground. The physio's room was a Portakabin, it was nothing fancy. It was so homely, the whole staff ate lunch at the same time. With the players and the staff, there was no us and them — we were all together.' McFadden was the definition of the Scottish term 'gallus': he had a swagger and an inner confidence about him that showed in the way he walked. He made that pretty clear when he lashed home a 40-yard screamer against France in Paris to clinch one of Scotland's most famous victories. McFadden also made headlines when he missed a team flight back from a tour of Hong Kong after spending the previous evening sampling the city's nightlife. He also had lots of kids copying his distinctive haircut, a garish red Mohawk, but even he was taken aback by Thomas.

'He was just a different kind of guy,' McFadden remembered. 'He was somebody in a group you'd try and avoid because he was so loud. It's so hard to describe him. He was the most hyper guy ever, all the time. One-on-one he was fine [but] in a group it was a nightmare. He'd do or say something. He had no filter — he was mental.' McFadden was also given an eye-opener into Thomas's strange frugality as he was still doing his cheap-car-in-the-winter routine. Now a Renault Megane had replaced the Micra, making it 15 different cars in four and a half years at Everton. But Thomas had now extended it to his boots, even though top players are given them for nothing and also likely to be paid to wear a certain brand. McFadden said, 'He'd have the latest boots but then in the winter he'd have on old leather boots, but he called them his winter shoes. He didn't have any outgoings and no bills. He rented Lee Carsley's flat, so he might have had his phone bill. He had no outgoings; he didn't like having stuff like that.'

It was true. Thomas had a two-bedroom flat in Liverpool city centre with the second one playing home to a pool table he'd transported over after getting it from sports shop Søren Søgaard A/S in Vejle. He could have bought a pool table in any number of outlets nearby in England, but his decision was an insight into how Thomas wanted to live and how he was always going to struggle to conform to the flash, glitzy world of professional football. He wanted his table from the shop he knew and felt a connection with. It showed that Thomas was a soul who lived for the moment without worrying about tomorrow, and felt most at ease in a controlled, tight-knit setting where he could just be himself.

The season was to be a memorable one for neutrals. Arsenal would win the title without losing a single game and subsequently be christened the Invincibles. Things weren't so rosy down at Goodison, where again every penny was a prisoner. The squad clearly wanted to go one better than the previous season and qualify for Europe. In terms of bolstering their numbers, they had McFadden and midfielder Kevin Kilbane, and Francis Jeffers returned on loan from Arsenal, where he'd struggled to make an impression. While they were all decent players, the league was stacked with massive names like Thierry Henry, John Terry, Frank Lampard, Steven Gerrard, Ashley Cole, Robbie Keane and Jay-Jay Okocha, all in their pomp. The sheer strength of Arsenal was an indication of how good a league it was then.

Everton were their first opponents and went down 2-1 before bouncing back to beat Fulham 3-1 and then earn a 2-2 draw with Charlton – talk about a mixed bag of a start! The spark of the previous season wasn't there. The team weren't digging in. During one spell in October and November, they went four games without even scoring.

Thomas wasn't firing on all cylinders, either. While he was still capable of producing moments of magic, they weren't as frequent and it seemed something had blunted his blade. Part of the reason was that his midfield rear gunner Carsley didn't play as much that season, meaning Thomas would have to be more disciplined, which of course he wasn't. When he tried to be, it frustrated him. It placed a greater burden on the rest of the team and the gamble backfired.

Another reason was that Wayne Rooney was now a certain starter. He played the most league games of any outfield player in the squad that season. Naturally, the manager was going to utilise such a potent weapon. Rooney was older and no longer a rookie and his regular inclusion meant the way the team played had changed. The shape wasn't the same and Thomas was no longer the fulcrum. That role had been handed to Rooney.

The switching of responsibility didn't cause any friction between the two star men, although a casual observer might have assumed they were trying to kill each other if they'd walked in during their 'shootout' one afternoon. Moyes said, 'It was the old gym, it's about 60 yards long. Him [Thomas] and Wayne, they were shooting fireworks at each other. They had big rockets full of gunpowder, they were holding one end and shooting them at each other.' The manager added, 'Tommy was mental in a good way. He was a great player and we loved him. He wouldn't listen but it wasn't in a bad way. I think it was a wee bit where he didn't want to hear you and just done [sic] his own thing. He was crazy in his training. He was a good lad but mental.'

Thomas didn't manage a goal until February, when he scored in a win over Aston Villa. His only other goal that season came against Newcastle United at St James' Park, where Everton went down 4-2. He ran on to a low cross, almost sliding as he connected with the ball, and fired it past Shay Given. Thomas didn't look happy. He reacted like a polite child opening a Christmas gift only to find a toy they didn't want. When Thomas scored that day he barely broke into a smile — that childlike enthusiasm wasn't there. Even his general play wasn't the same. He looked frustrated and didn't seem to be enjoying himself as much as he had. It wasn't the Thomas everyone knew.

Everton noticeably felt the absence of his spark. Not even Moyes, despite being an astute manager, could relight the fire in Thomas or the team in general. Relegation had become a real threat and Everton fans found themselves back in the same hellish déjà-vu situation they'd been in two years earlier, when Walter and Archie were sacked. The thought of going down was unthinkable. With TV income so high and only increasing, any team who was relegated would have to drastically slash their budgets.

To compound things, competition was so fierce that there was no guarantee of being promoted straight back to the Premier League. Quite simply, going down could mean decades in the doldrums. Money would go, budgets would be chainsawed and star players would leave – it was a vicious cycle.

In the end, Everton clung on for dear life and finished 17th, narrowly above the relegation places, as Leicester City, Leeds United and Wolverhampton Wanderers fell through the trapdoor into oblivion. It had been far too close for comfort but at least Moyes, the players and the fans could breathe a sigh of relief and look ahead to the summer, when they could get their house back in order. They couldn't have had two more contrasting seasons and needed to work out how to get back to what they'd been doing best.

Before then, Thomas had the tonic of heading off to Euro 2004 with Denmark. He never had to worry about his place in the squad and was handed his customary number seven jersey. Now aged 28, he was one of the more experienced players, so there was a burden on him not only to perform but to help the newer boys adjust to the do-or-die nature of knockout football at the highest level.

But regular as clockwork, Thomas once again ended up in the headlines before a major tournament for reasons that had nothing to do with football.

The Danish squad had a farewell meal with their wives and partners before flying out to Portugal. It took place in Copenhagen's Café Ketchup, which had made front-page news a few years earlier when Tøfting had reportedly got into an argument over loud singing and assaulted the manager, resulting in a four-month jail sentence. Thomas had been there with his team-mate that night but wasn't involved in the rumpus or any violence.

This gathering, of course, didn't feature Tøfting as he'd since retired from international football, but once again *SE og HØR* magazine were watching the goings-on closely. They noticed that while all the wives and girlfriends had arrived and were enjoying the festivities, there was no sign of Gitte. They began probing why; after all she was a fellow footballer, so would surely be interested in seeing her childhood sweetheart and the rest of the players off to a tournament they had justified high hopes of doing well in.

It transpired that Gitte had moved back to Vejle to train as a nurse and while they had stayed together initially, their relationship was now over. It was the reason Thomas was in turmoil; he is an individual who craves routine, community, familiarity and closeness. Here was the girl he'd been with since he was 17 and who'd followed him to Hamburg and Liverpool, supporting him to the hilt. She was no longer there and Thomas was on his own. The reason why his performances had dipped had become clear. Being criticised by the media for his play or facing superstars didn't bother Thomas, but when it came to his close personal circle he couldn't handle trauma or disruption. Just as he'd had Fritsen and le Fevre guiding him during games, he'd had Gitte with him off the pitch to provide support and understanding. When questioned about the split, his agent John Sivebæk was quoted in the Danish press as saying, 'Thomas does not want to talk publicly about it right now. He feels it's too private.'

The lid being lifted seemed to unburden Thomas and at least meant he didn't have to bottle it up as everyone in Denmark now knew about it. The squad arrived at their training base in Portimão, part of the Algarve region, engulfed by the usual media storm, but Olsen rallied round and got them focused on their jobs.

Their group contained Sweden, Bulgaria and big guns Italy, who they'd face first in Guimarães. Thomas wasn't available for selection as he'd done his usual trick of mixing genius and stupidity in the final qualifier against Bosnia and Herzegovina. He had laid Denmark's goal on a silver platter for Jorgensen by slipping a cheeky pass through a bamboozled defender's legs –4 it was pure poetry like Michael Jackson effortlessly pulling off a moonwalk. But later in the match, showing his trademark disregard for stopping and thinking first, Thomas picked up a needless second booking and was sent off for simply being too focused on playing every single second at maximum tempo. So against Italy, he had to sit frustrated on the sidelines. It was a talented Italian side, from keeper Gianluigi Buffon to Cannavaro in defence and creative stars like Del Piero and Francesco Totti pulling the strings higher up. But the Danes were organised, resolute and kept it goalless.

Then it was on to Braga to play Bulgaria and Thomas was back in, replacing Christian Poulsen. Now with their playmaker back, the Danes could look to be more expansive and do some damage in an attacking sense. In the last match they'd been hampered like turning up to a gunfight brandishing a knife but with Thomas now free of the pressure of having to hide his split with Gitte, he was as sharp as a tack – he was sucking diesel during that match. His controlled passing and smarts ripped the Bulgarians to shreds; they just couldn't handle him. Just before half time, he delivered yet another killer pass that allowed Jørgensen to unselfishly set up Tomasson to roll the ball into an empty net. Thomas kept it going, dictating the pace of the match and controlling the tempo with ease as Denmark got a second to run out 2-0 winners.

Their final group game was in Porto and is still regarded as one of the most controversial international matches. It was dubbed 'The Scandi Stitch-Up' and so called because of the way results transpired. Sweden and Denmark would qualify at the expense of Italy if they shared the points in a high-scoring draw. Before the game even kicked off, there were conspiracy theories floating around mainly in the Italian media and vicious rumours abounded. Denmark boss Olsen said, 'That's ridiculous. Don't speak about that. We are honest people. We are going out to win the game and that's all. They [Italy] can speak about these things but not Denmark and Sweden. We are going honestly for a result.' One of Sweden's coaching staff, Lars Lagerbäck, added, 'Machiavelli might have been Italian and Italians might like to think in a Machiavellian way, but it would not be possible to play for a 2-2 draw against Denmark and I don't think it will end 2-2 — that is a very unusual result.'

Of course, at the end of the game, to the shock horror of many neutrals and all Italians, it *was* 2-2. Both teams took the field in awful, wet, windy conditions. Denmark had taken the lead with Thomas in imperious form, head and shoulders above everyone else. Even with Zlatan Ibrahimović in the Swedish team, it was Thomas who was the star man as he waltzed around showing world-class skills and delivering smart passes. It's not an exaggeration to say he was even above this level at that point in his career – he was way better than Sweden's midfield, who were all solid pros. An article in leading football magazine *FourFourTwo* highlighted the exasperation of the Swedes at how well Thomas was playing. One of their brassed-off players, Anders Andersson, reportedly shouted at him, 'Come on, bloody hell, give us a break now,' to which Thomas replied, 'Yes, but then you have to at least go forward.' The account gave the conspiracy theorists even more traction. With only a few minutes left, Sweden scored a second equaliser to send both Scandinavian countries through and Italy home. AC Milan director Adriano Galliani ranted, 'We got as many points as the players who are blond and beautiful. But we are darker and not as beautiful.'

Denmark marched on to the quarter-finals to face the Czech Republic , who were a special team at the time with

Pavel Nedvěd, Karel Poborský, Milan Baroš and 6ft 7in beanpole striker Jan Koller. Even with Thomas flying, it was a tough ask as the Czech players were all skilful, good on the ball and playing at the top level. Most importantly, they knew how to win games. Thomas was simply outgunned; even he couldn't take on an entire midfield of class acts. The Danes went down 3-0, conceding all the goals in the second half.

Thomas left Portugal having proved he was a match for anyone on his day. Although he didn't know it at the time, he would not play in a major international tournament again. There was something else he didn't know: that he was on the verge of one of the most surprising transfers of all time. It was to shock fans, journalists and team-mates — and to be frank even Thomas himself.

Chapter 11

Vamos Real!

WAYNE Rooney was the key in Thomas finally getting to the summit of the game. It was a knock-on effect, starting with Rooney's fantastic Euro 2004, where he proved he was sheer world class despite being just 18. He banged in four goals and put in a string of extremely impressive performances for England under the stewardship of Sven-Goran Eriksson. A club like Everton, without the money to pay top wages and also in need of cash, were always going to be fighting a losing battle to keep Rooney. There were plenty of suitors as scouts marvelled at how the young prodigy made seasoned professionals look like novices on the international stage. Sir Alex Ferguson was the one who grabbed Rooney's attention and he moved to Manchester United for an initial £20 million, which was set to rise to £27 million depending on appearances. It transpired to be money well spent: Rooney left Old Trafford in 2017 as the leading scorer in the club's history with 253 goals.

Moving in the other direction was striker Marcus Bent and attacking Australian midfielder Tim Cahill, who joined from south London side Millwall. Radzinski also left the club but apart from that it was pretty much the same team that took up the mantle.

After such a horrendous previous season, there was a clear determination to make sure 2004/05 was going to be better. A major factor was that what had inhibited them before was now not an issue as they no longer had to revolve the team around Rooney. He had been a dominant figure due to the media hype and the adulation of fans, many of whom looked at the teenager as a son. But for those reasons and a few others, it had disrupted the finely balanced chemistry of Everton's great season two years earlier.

Now they could pick up where they had left off at the end of 2002/03, and almost pretend the previous season never happened, airbursh it from their minds . Thomas was reinstated as the team's match-winner, the guy to be creative, to take on the responsibility and be the fulcrum. Also, his partner Carsley played more games than the season before and the two of them took to being back in tandem like ducks to water. All the elements came together like a perfect storm to create the ideal platform for Thomas to showcase his ability. To prove the point, he got off to a flyer in the season opener against Arsenal as Thomas clipped a sublime chip for Carsley to score. Everton still lost 4-1 but Thomas kept his rich vein of form going following Euro 2004. He had put the break-up with Gitte behind him, resumed his favoured on-field role and was back in the zone.

In the next match away to Crystal Palace, Thomas scored twice and created the other for Bent as Everton won 3-1. Next followed a 2-1 win over West Bromwich Albion, Leon Osman's opening goal coming from a long-range throw by Thomas. At this point, he really was doing it all.

Normally, flair players don't do the mundane things like taking throw-ins but that was Thomas. He wanted to have the ball all the time in any scenario. Plus his hulking physique meant he had a good arm with which to launch the ball. He'd matured on the pitch and was really playing some scintillating stuff. By the end of October, Everton were sitting pretty in third and it was no coincidence that Thomas was back as the main man and playing with a partner who understood what he required to flourish.

But that didn't mean he wasn't still up to his old antics. He might have been playing out of his skin but Thomas was still Thomas. Kevin Kilbane spoke about Thomas's continued love of fireworks, which goes back to his days at Hamburg. 'He was a lunatic,' Kilbane said. 'There was a bit of drainpipe that had come loose at the training ground and Thomas was using that as a rocket launcher to fire rockets out of the drainpipe across the training ground. Gravesen had a screw loose somewhere along the line.' But even allowing for his outlandish behaviour, Kilbane admits that Thomas was the key element for Everton at that time. 'He was a brilliant, brilliant footballer who was certainly underrated,' Kilbane admitted. 'Honestly, a class player. You had to let him go [and] do his own thing on the pitch. When we started to do well in my second season, Moyes put Gravesen as a number ten and just said "go play, do what you want". He was also the strongest man in the world, I am talking ridiculously strong. He never did a weight, never went in the gym. The fitness coach would try [and] get him [in] the gym and he'd have none of it. He'd wrestle lads, get them on the floor and you couldn't move — he was a big kid.'

Everton's good form continued with Thomas roaming the pitch, playing with the freedom he craved. They went seven games unbeaten, including a 1-0 win over Liverpool in the Merseyside derby and a 2-1 victory against Manchester City, in which Cahill scored from a perfectly flighted free kick by Thomas before Bent headed in after another peach of a delivery by Mad Dog. Cahill, in particular, was making Thomas's work look more obvious as he was a tireless runner who'd often break from midfield. In fact, Cahill was almost a deep-lying striker and finished the season with 11 league goals. He was the ideal outlet for Thomas's vision and passing ability. But despite his great play, Thomas's team-mates were still struggling to get to grips with him. Osman said, 'He was even crazier than whatever you've heard. You could be walking down the corridor and you'd be scared of making eye contact with him. He was playful — when he was in the right mood — but you didn't want to look him in the eye because the next thing you knew, he'd be wrestling with you on the floor. He's a one-off. You just never knew what he was going to do next.'

By the turn of the year Everton had reached the dizzy heights of a Champions League place, which was beyond the club's wildest dreams. They'd gone on another superb streak of eight games without defeat. Everton had no right to be challenging but on 28 December, they had the chance to go even higher into second. Considering their resources and previous form, here they were now keeping pace with megabucks Chelsea, who'd go on to become champions at the end of the season with a record haul of 95 points in the Special One José Mourinho's first year in charge. Mourinho had been bankrolled by Roman Abramovich and was able to sign household names. It meant he had such strength in depth that he could afford to rotate his squad to keep them fresh. By contrast, Everton were a small squad, with everyone playing to the max and straining to keep it going.

But the wheels were about to come off. On 4 January , Thomas played his last game for Everton. He left his mark on the final game, as he sent over yet another glorious corner for Alan Stubbs to smash home as the Toffees beat Portsmouth 2-1. Thomas had played 141 times for Everton, almost three times the amount of appearances he'd made for Vejle and more than double the number he'd clocked up at HSV.

His contract was due to run out in the summer of 2005 and considering his inspirational form, it wasn't a surprise that word had spread about what a bargain could be snapped up for a relatively low price. Due to the Bosman ruling, a player becomes a free agent when their contract finishes and can move for no transfer fee. As their contract winds down, their value drops drastically. The newspapers reported that AC Milan and Manchester United were circling with an eye on putting in a bid, but still no one expected what was about to play out.

A jaw-dropping deal appeared totally out of the blue as it was announced in mid-January that Thomas had signed for the most glamorous club on the planet, Real Madrid. He'd gone for £2.6 million, which was actually a profit for Everton, but his true value was far higher. The club had to accept that or face getting nothing in the summer.

It was the opportunity of a lifetime, going from a team targeting mid-table safety in England to a global megaclub with fans on every continent who expected to win every single trophy they competed for. On paper, it was a no-brainer, with his weekly salary reported to be £73,000, but even his team-mates were taken aback by how quickly the move came about. Stubbs said: 'We all knew what Thomas's ability was, but was it a surprise? Yes.'

The Everton squad also began to detect that despite wanting to go and test himself against the world's best players, Thomas didn't want to leave the cosy and homely environment he had become part of. He'd split up with Gitte, now he was leaving a club that was big, but not massive. He felt at ease there, part of a community similar to the one he'd been raised in back in Vejle. He knew everyone and they knew him. He wasn't someone who was attracted by bright lights, despite his eccentricity.

Everton captain David Weir recalled how a private plane was waiting on the tarmac to fly Thomas over to Spain, but he seemed to be stalling about leaving the training ground for the final time. Weir said, 'I think he wanted to go but he was very settled at Everton and I think he enjoyed the atmosphere. He was probably torn about going to a massive club and all the attractions of that, but I got the impression he wasn't sure and seemed reticent. You're stepping into the world stage there. He was very talented, though, so we knew he could handle the football side of things.'

The Santiago Bernabéu Stadium in Madrid had played host to every type of player in its long, illustrious history, but even it hadn't seen anyone quite like Mad Dog.

Chapter 12

He's a Galáctico

ANY football transfer is a sliding-doors moment for both the team that's left behind and the club the player is joining. With Thomas's move, it's pretty telling to look at it in that manner. The stone-cold facts put any naysayers in their place.

With him in the team, Everton won 13 games and drew four of their opening 22 fixtures. Without him, they won five of their remaining 16 and lost eight. Side by side, with Thomas the win rate was 59 per cent and without him, it fell to 27 per cent.

Thankfully, because of their superb run up until January with Thomas in the team, Everton managed to hang on to fourth spot and earn a place in the Champions League qualifying round. That was a huge achievement for the coaching staff and all the players. At time of writing 13 years later, the team has yet to better that position, despite now being majority-owned by Iranian billionaire Farhad Moshiri and spending vast sums such as £40 million on Icelandic midfielder Gylfi Sigurðsson and signing Brazilian striker Richarlison in a £50 million deal.

Before he was unveiled in Madrid, an eyebrow-raising theory about Thomas coursed around the football world. It was that Madrid were looking for a midfielder to act as a defensive shield in their Los Galácticos team, who all seemed to focus on scoring highlight reel-style goals. They'd lost their much-heralded deep-lying midfielder Claude Makélélé to Chelsea 18 months earlier. The small Frenchman was a pioneer. So much so that his sitting role in midfield, where he'd stop attacks by pouncing and stealing the ball then feed a pass to his team's attackers, was named in the game as the Makélélé role. Soon, every team in Europe had someone playing the Makélélé position, although very few managed it as proficiently because of the very specific skillset required. The key to it was discipline; the player would have to hold their position even when the ball was further upfield. They had to resist the urge to go forward and anticipate where the opposing team might attack from. The player in the Makélélé role had to be there, win the ball back with a minimum of fuss and spark another attacking wave.

In black and white, it was all the things Thomas wasn't. He had skills that had impressed all of his previous team-mates; he could use both feet, dribble, take great corners and hit rocket shots. But sticking to a particular position was alien to him. Weir said, 'He definitely had the ability, there was no doubt about that. But the role they were looking for was a defensive role. He wasn't that player. It wasn't a surprise that they signed him as he was a really talented player. It was more of a surprise the role they were looking for him to fill.'

That sentiment was echoed by Danish international Morten Wieghorst, who added, 'When he went to Madrid and they saw him as a holding midfielder, a few people thought, "Maybe that's not him." I mean who would turn down the chance to go? But to ask him to do it? He would do it to get in the team, but it wasn't the best role for him. He'd do anything to get on the ball.'

What began circulating around the rumour mill and fan forums was that Madrid had made a monumental mistake. They'd been coming to Everton and scouting their games, and were impressed with this bald, stocky, strong midfielder. But there were two of them: number 16 Thomas Gravesen and his partner in the middle of the park, number 26 Lee Carsley.

Quite a few commentators reckoned that they'd actually got them confused and weren't sure who was who. The theory was they'd seen Carsley's defensive skills and thought that's who they were getting for their £2.6 million. They had seemingly bought a square peg for a round hole - The *Liverpool Echo* ran the headline: 'Bald truth is, Madrid have got the wrong man'.

Once they clapped eyes on him, Madrid didn't back out and completed the deal as normal. Everton used all the leverage they could to get the highest price and negotiated an option to back him back, plus a 20 per cent sell-on fee. Once all the paperwork was done, Madrid presented him to the world's media, Thomas penned a three-and-a-half-year deal and was given his favoured number 16 shirt. Club president Florentino Perez did nothing to keep it low-key and predicted Thomas would be the missing piece in their puzzle. He raved, 'We have signed Denmark's best player — and that's not me saying that. His national team coach said so. He has proven himself in the German and English leagues. He is, without doubt, the player we were missing.'

That certainly was some statement as this was the most glamorous and talked-about club squad of all time in football — anywhere. Real Madrid were the most successful team in Europe and had at that time nine Champions Leagues to their name and 29 Spanish league titles since forming back in 1902. They even feature the Spanish royal crown on their badge after it was bestowed to the club by King Alfonso XIII.

It was also at the peak of the Los Galácticos era, which was an initiative by Real Madrid where every summer they'd sign a global superstar and put them all together in one squad. It was akin to a young kid playing on his PlayStation and putting all his favourite stars in the same team. As it was such an iconic club, the players were happy to be part of the project, when usually they'd be the dominant figure at one club and be able to rule the roost. This was Hollywood FC. Lights, camera, action!

In goal was Iker Casillas, one of the continent's best goalkeepers since bursting on to the scene in his teens, the full-backs were Michel Salgado and Brazilian Roberto Carlos, known for his thundering free kicks and strapping tree-trunk thighs that powered him up and down the left side of football pitches for decades. The centre of defence contained Ivan Helguera and Walter Samuel, both rugged and far from shrinking violets.

In the attacking department, it's hard to imagine their strikers could have been of a higher pedigree. They featured the original Ronaldo, who'd scored 30 goals or more in his last two years at Madrid, even when he wasn't in great shape due to a catalogue of injuries.

But he was tip-top and back in prime condition, and was flying at the point Thomas arrived. Goal machine Michael Owen was also there, along with club captain Raul, who was regarded as one of Spain's best ever players. It's not hard to understand why: Raul scored 228 goals in 500 games at the very top level.

As if that wasn't enough, Madrid's strongest department was their awe-inspiring midfield. It had puzzled observers wondering how on earth Thomas was going to force his way in. These superstars had to play or they'd agitate for a move away. That was all part of the Los Galácticos formula: they all accommodated each other's egos but they all played.

On the right-hand side was the world's best-known player David Beckham, who was by this time also a cultural and fashion icon. In the centre was the best player of his generation, the masterful Zinedine Zidane, who'd moved to Madrid for a world-record €77.5 million. He was a player who could do anything with the ball, sometimes seemingly defying the laws of gravity. Alongside him in the middle was Guti, who was then the club's vice-captain and a massive favourite with the fans; he stayed for his entire career and won 15 trophies. Completing the midfield was the Portuguese technician Luis Figo, who'd crossed the bitter divide from Barcelona to Real Madrid — they're deadly rivals as Spain's biggest teams — for what was then a world-record €62 million fee, now surpassed by his team-mate.

At the press conference to unveil Thomas, Florentino Perez also said, 'He has had many chances to go to other clubs, Italians or English, but he has ruled out any option that was not playing in Madrid.' In typical Thomas style, with no filter and without the remotest idea how to play the media, he said he hadn't had any other offers and that it was only Madrid who had got in contact. He was clearly going to need a few pointers in self-promotion from his new Hollywood FC pals.

Nevertheless, he had joined and was now one of Los Galácticos. It had capped an amazing journey from rural Denmark to playing alongside the planet's most famous, heralded and talented players.

Thomas would be strutting his stuff in the Santiago Bernabéu, which at that time held 80,354 supporters — almost double the entire population of Vejle. In the world of football, there was no grander stage and Thomas was arriving at the peak of glitz, glamour and hype. One of the most combustible characters in the game was about to suit up and go into football's most potent pressure cooker. Predicting how it would unfold was impossible.

Watching on from afar was Thomas's former assistant manager at Everton, Archie Knox, who first brought him over to England. Knox said, 'We always got on well. I can remember phoning him when he got the move to Real Madrid. I called him and said, "Is that Thomas Gravesen of Real Madrid?" And he said, "I can't believe it myself." I said, "That makes two of us."'

Even with an endless amount written about the Madrid squad, from Beckham's newspaper-hogging fashion sense to Zidane's graceful tricks and a multitude of other issues swirling around the squad, the media in Spain took a shine to Thomas. They took a shine to his honesty and instinctive way of conducting himself. According to the newspapers, Mad Dog had now become *El Ogro*, The Ogre – the man-eating monster. Before he'd even made it on to the pitch, he'd been given that new nickname, sowing the seeds of cult hero status yet again, but this time in the midst of superstars in Spain's glamorous capital. Honest *El Ogro* admitted: 'At the beginning I asked myself: "What are you doing here?"'

Chapter 13

Dentist Thomas

NOT only were Los Galácticos the most famous and glamorous stars in the game, they were also extremely successful. They had more medals in their cupboards than Fort Knox.

Casillas had won the Champions League twice. Roberto Carlos had three Champions Leagues, three Spanish leagues and had a World Cup to his name. Figo had four Spanish league crowns, a Champions League, a UEFA Cup Winners' Cup and a UEFA Super Cup. Beckham had won six English Premier League titles, two FA Cups and a Champions League. Zidane had won both the World Cup and European Championships with France, along with two Italian leagues and a Spanish title. He was also a three-time World Player of the Year. Ronaldo had two World Cups, a UEFA Cup Winners' Cup, a UEFA Cup and two Spanish league title medals in his cabinet, plus he was another three-time World Player of the Year. Owen was a previous Ballon d'Or recipient, which then was awarded to the European Footballer of the Year, along with an FA Cup and UEFA Cup.

There was nothing these players hadn't won. They were serial winners of the game's biggest prizes. It was reported that Thomas later marched along to the dressing room for the first time and while the squad of modern-day legends was getting ready for training, he stood in the doorway and loudly proclaimed, 'I am your saviour.'

Thomas subsequently denied the story, claiming, 'Those stories were not true; anyone who knows me can see that. I just walked in and said, "Hello, I'm Thomas." In the beginning you watch, you learn and you don't go round shouting. I wouldn't ever, ever come in saying I'm a saviour.'

Forty-eight hours after signing, Thomas made his bow in the famous all-white kit. Real Zaragoza were the visitors to the Santiago Bernabéu and they shocked everyone by taking the lead after 22 minutes, David Villa firing them ahead. Just before half-time, skipper Raul pulled the home team level before Ronaldo made it 2-1 ten minutes after the restart. Then, on 68 minutes, the fourth official hoisted the substitutes' board to signal Madrid's number seven was coming off. Going the other way was Thomas, replacing the maestro Figo. He acquitted himself well and Owen added a third, making it a satisfying game for all concerned. Thomas was off and running and was now officially a Galáctico. He'd joined the most exclusive members' club in football.

Spanish sports newspaper *Marca* welcomed Thomas in typical tabloid fashion by plastering him across its front page in lurid bright green, mocking him up as the Mike Myers-voiced animated hero *Shrek*.

After the game, Thomas wowed, 'It is a truly fantastic feeling and I am happy and proud. It is a very big day for me and I got a fantastic welcome from the fans, which really helped me. I was tense and nervous before the match and didn't really expect to get on the pitch.' Just like his former team-mates had revealed, Thomas had no real ties in Liverpool and explained how easy it had been to move his life to another country in a matter of hours. 'I didn't have time to pack anything, to do anything,' he added. 'The only reason I sold my car was I was going to sell it anyway. I arrived, was presented, trained and then we had a game the day after.'

After the dust had settled, and the excitement had died down, it was on to the serious business of trying to carve out a regular place in the team. In Madrid, the boardroom hierarchy exerts a lot of influence on the playing personnel, so sometimes managers might not have wanted a Galáctico but didn't have the authority to block it. It wasn't because they weren't all great players because they certainly were; it was because they might not suit the system or tactical plan. It was like moving house and trying to squeeze your boxes into a lightning-fast but cramped Lamborghini. But that's not how it worked in Madrid. It was a case of the manager being told from above: 'You're getting this superstar to join all the others and we want them to play, as that's our brand and the fans love it.'

The team's manager was Brazilian Vanderlei Luxemburgo, who'd had a 25-year career in South America, including a spell in charge of his country. He'd only taken over at Madrid two weeks before Thomas signed, so it was highly unlikely that he'd come up with the idea to do the deal. There simply wouldn't have been enough time to go in to Real, assess the team, plan out what was needed and then look around to see who fitted the bill. Thomas had been spotted by those further up the chain, hence the gushing comments from Florentino Pérez. It's not normal for a club's board member to talk about new signings, that's the manager's department.

But no one walked through the doors at Real Madrid without the say so of Pérez; he was the man signing the cheques. But he was also keen to attract players who would whip up the supporters, get them excited and up off their seats. The way to play in Madrid was with style, passion and flair, all characteristics that Thomas had in abundance, so he was Pérez's kind of player, without doubt. Then there was also the director of football, Italian tactical mastermind Arrigo Sacchi. He was the man who created the dominant AC Milan team of the late 1980s featuring the three great Dutchmen Marco van Basten, Ruud Gullit and Frank Rijkaard. His system at that time was predicated on a tough, stingy defence shepherded by Franco Baresi alongside

A fresh-faced Thomas with childhood sweetheart and fellow footballer Gitte Pedersen back in Vejle.

The legendary Danish manager Ole Fritsen who Thomas refers to as his mentor.

Thomas playing for German giants HSV, his first step on the ladder of European football.

It wasn't long before Thomas was a cult hero at Everton thanks to intensity like this.

Always a proud Dane, Thomas gave his all in the red and white of his country, winning 66 caps.

Thomas shows Steven Gerrard who's boss in another pulsating Merseyside derby.

Mad Dog and Lee Carsley were blood brothers on and off the pitch. In fact, some people reckon Real Madrid wanted Lee but got him confused with Thomas.

The attention of the world's media was something Thomas never enjoyed and he eventually refused to engage with them.

Everton boss David Moyes was not the first – or last – manager to end up frustrated with Thomas's all-consuming love of chasing the ball all over the pitch.

Iron Mike Tyson saw a kindred spirit in Thomas, demanding his shirt which he wore with pride.

Beckham and Thomas. The two number 7s were their country's biggest stars and became team-mates in Spain.

'Little Thomas' is captured inadvertently by Danish photographer Nils Meilvang as he takes a picture of Claus Jensen, during a training session ahead of a Euro 2004 qualifier in Romania.

In true Thomas style, as he signs for the world's most glamorous club – he looks anything but happy.

Thomas surprised many by being able to hold his own in Madrid alongside Los Galácticos.

In another bitter inter-city rivalry, Thomas rises to the occasion and lets Atlético Madrid's Fernando Torres know there's a new sheriff in town.

Not overawed by the superstars he was surrounded by, Thomas was vocal and confident in Madrid. Here he is telling World Cup winner Roberto Carlos what to do.

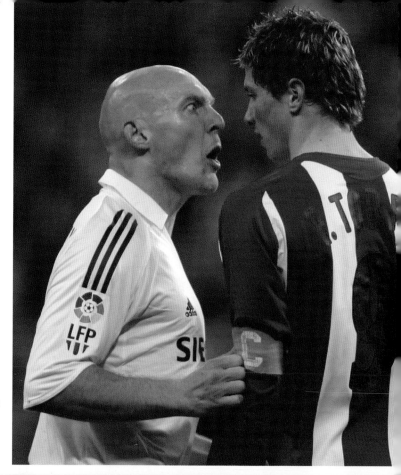

Billed as the biggest club game on the planet – El Clásico, Real vs Barcelona. Thomas gets to grips with Brazilian genius Ronaldinho in what was part of an individual display that's still marvelled at by Real fans today.

Going to Real allowed Thomas the chance to grace the Champions League. Here he is closing down Zlatan Ibrahimović as two heavyweights of the game, Madrid and Juventus, slug it out.

Thomas led Denmark to a crushing win over France at the 2002 World Cup. He dominated the game and even had the great Zidane in his pocket that afternoon.

Celtic gaffer Gordon Strachan and Thomas never seemed to be on the same wavelength. Here's the manager giving Mad Dog a bollocking during a Champions League clash.

Another white-hot derby match this time in Glasgow and Thomas is in the thick of the action, with Rangers skipper Barry Ferguson. But they'd be having a very different conversation at half-time.

Alessandro Costacurta, Mauro Tassotti and Paolo Maldini. While Sacchi's Milan side were far from boring, they were very well organised and playing a position rigidly as that part of the team was key. You didn't go floating around the pitch under Sacchi and if you did you'd be sitting beside him on the bench in the next game.

So it's puzzling why Sacchi suggested to Pérez that he make a move for Thomas — if indeed he did so. Maybe Pérez did it all himself. Mad Dog's Everton team-mate David Weir had his own theory. 'Thomas was the sort of fella if you gave him an exact, specific role, he'd follow it to the letter but if there was any leeway, he'd take the licence to use it and go to the opposite extreme,' Weir said. 'It was either to the letter of the law or the complete opposite.' So perhaps master tactician Sacchi thought that if Thomas was told to do just one thing in explicit detail, he'd do it and block everything else out. It's not that strange a theory as since his days as a boy back in Vejle, people had spoken of his blinding tunnel vision and almost obsessive compulsion once he got attached to something. He had it with cars, playing pool, the *Call of Duty* video game. Once he got something into his head, it was damn near impossible to get it out and he'd throw himself into it with every fibre of his being. Weir added, 'He had that obsessive nature. You would see if he was playing a game or something, he would be obsessive with it and spend the time he needed to get the results. If you get him fixated on something, he'd practice, practice, practice.'

Thomas also spoke in Spain about how he was spending his days off watching around nine hours of football a day, catching games from different leagues around the world. He added, 'I have no other passion in life. My passion is football, I like to play it, watch it, talk about it, and I like to train. Taking care of yourself is very important, being strong is fundamental, eating well in the right way, especially pasta, and if I eat meat, it's chicken and fish, and vegetables.'

With the whirlwind having passed, Thomas had to assimilate into the Madrid squad and become one of the lads. No longer was it the homely training complex he'd been used to at Everton, where he'd be using portable rooms, and eating together with the non-playing staff every day. During Thomas's spell, the Real squad initially trained at their Las Rozas base before months later moving to Ciudad Real Madrid (Real Madrid City), a huge 8,300-square metre venue with 57 rooms, a cinema, a climate-controlled pool and a reception area. That was on top of the 12 individual pitches, some of which were synthetic and some natural grass.

There was also a multitude of rehab facilities, including a hydrotherapy centre with hot and cold pools. This was like nothing Thomas had ever seen; money was no object at this club. Everything was laid on for the superstars to perform at their peak. Borja Fernández, who was part of the squad, reiterated how intense it was, saying 'everything at Real Madrid is accelerated'.

Thomas was undoubtedly one of Europe's leading midfielders at that point due to his performances for both Everton and Denmark. Now it was an intriguing question of how good he could become with these facilities at his disposal and players of such high calibre to spur him on. Anyone who thought Thomas was going to Madrid just to pick up a big salary was in for a shock. Thomas was going there to play. He still only had one gear, the same one he had back in his days in the youth team at Vejle, and that was full steam ahead, no matter what obstacles appeared.

In training Thomas was his usual boisterous self, flying into tackles and putting maximum effort into every single second as if his life depended on it. But he also brought his sporadic poor judgement to Spain too and would think nothing of grabbing and putting any of the Galácticos in one of his bone-crushing bear hugs. Of course, even they couldn't get out of them, no matter how long they'd spent in the gym. Borja Fernández added, 'Thomas was a character, he made us laugh a lot. He was so much fun and genuine too.'

He went a bit too far, though, when he decided to throw around the world's top striker, Ronaldo, who was worshipped by millions and an icon to people everywhere. You can imagine the horror on the management team's faces when they saw their main source of goals, who was worth his weight in gold, in the unforgiving hands of the Ogre. Despite being 6ft tall and rippling with muscles, Ronaldo for all his might couldn't get loose and ended up being tossed around like a rag doll. After some rough and tumble, the shenanigans ended with Ronaldo lying there minus a tooth. The incident, of course, made the papers. While there was no malice or fallout, it showed that Thomas wasn't going to tone down his antics. Even if he was playing for the biggest club in the world, he was still going to have a hell of a lot of fun doing it.

Thomas's Danish team-mate Morten Wieghorst said, 'In Spain, they wouldn't have experienced many players like him and that's why at Real Madrid that stuff came out about his old tricks, so to speak. They weren't used to that kind of character and to be fair, neither were we.' It wasn't to be the last time Thomas man-handled a Brazilian team-mate, but the next incident wouldn't be so light-hearted.

Thomas was in the starting line-up for Madrid's next game, a home clash with Real Mallorca, which they won comfortably 3-1, thanks to goals from Figo, Samuel and Santiago Solari. Michael Owen was a substitute that day and replaced Thomas with 16 minutes to go. Thomas acquitted himself well but picked up a yellow card. Luxemburgo clearly liked what he'd seen as Thomas retained his place and played the full match away to Numancia, with Beckham and Salgado scoring to give Madrid the win. The momentum kept going and Espanyol were given a 4-0 thumping, with the final goal of the match being Thomas's first and only in all white. The ball broke to him on the edge of the penalty box and he side-footed a precise shot low into the corner of the net, displaying flawless technique. Then he turned, raised both his arms in the air and saluted the 70,959 fans in attendance.

Madrid then travelled to Osasuna and beat them 2-1 thanks to goals from Owen and Helguera. Thomas was in dreamland; he'd been part of an incredible transfer, he was in the team at Real Madrid of all places, he'd scored and now he'd been part of a record achievement. The Osasuna game meant Madrid had won seven on the spin, which tied a club record. The party vibe ended in the very next match though, as Madrid went down to Athletic Bilbao, an interesting team with a rule of only signing and playing Basque players. While on paper the 2-0 defeat looked a shock result, there was more to it. Madrid were due to play a massive Champions League game against Juventus a few days later. It was their target for the season as they were struggling to keep pace with Barcelona in the league. As a result, Zidane, Ronaldo and Raul were all rested and Bilbao capitalised on their weakened opponents. Despite the disappointment, it was quickly forgotten about in Madrid and all eyes turned to European football's biggest prize.

Chapter 14

Mission Complete

TODAY'S generation of players all dream of being in the Champions League. It's the strongest competition anywhere, and arguably even harder to win than the World Cup. With the vast riches sloshing around, Europe's clubs are able to sign the best players no matter where they come from. You don't face one star man and his supporting cast, you end up facing Stallone, Schwarzenegger and Willis all at the same time. Lionel Messi is a great example. He's from Argentina and regarded by many as the greatest player ever, but he's been at Barcelona for his entire career surrounded by world-class operators. There are no passengers in the upper echelons of the European game.

No player takes it lightly to line up on a Champions League night; it's something they dream of from the moment they first play football as a kid. The moment it hits them is when both teams stand on the pitch, looking back at the crowd in front of the cameras, and that spine-tingling classical anthem starts up. The hairs on the back of everyone's neck stand up and the adrenaline starts to pump.

Now it was happening for Thomas. If he'd stayed at Everton, he'd have been preparing for a trip to Aston Villa in England's second biggest city, Birmingham. But here he was in a crackling Bernabéu, set to pit his wits against the cream at the very top level.

All the stars were refreshed and back in the Madrid team along with Thomas, and together they were preparing to face Turin giants Juventus. Due to a colour clash, the Italians were resplendent in their blue away kit and their team contained the likes of Ibrahimović, Pavel Nedvěd, Del Piero, Thuram, Mauro Camoranesi and Fabio Cannavaro. It didn't get any better. Two juggernauts driven by top operators about to collide over the course of two games. With the home fans putting the wind in their sails, Madrid laid siege to the Italians' goal, spurred on by Zidane and Beckham, who were both supplying clever balls. They scored with a header from Helguera but despite dominating the game and Juventus having their moments too, it remained 1-0 at full time. It had been a pulsating, dynamic game full of strength, power, skill and pace, the sort that makes the Champions League so popular, the best players going at it hammer and tongs.

Thomas dovetailed well with his superstar team-mates. He'd been spraying passes around and did not look remotely out of place. All the assertions from past team-mates and coaches about how good he was were turning out to be accurate. Even more shocking was the fact he seemed to be listening to the manager, playing his position and working for the team in a role no one thought he could.

Before the return leg, Madrid had league business to attend to and squared up to Real Betis at the Bernabéu. Still flying after their great victory over Juventus, they won 3-1 with Thomas once again looking comfortable and accomplished in midfield. Real followed that up with a 1-1 draw at Valencia's Mestalla Stadium. Two weeks after the 1-0 win in Madrid, Juventus and Real faced off again in the second leg at Turin's Stadio delle Alpi. This time there were 68,650 supporters inside the stadium, eagerly welcoming the teams as they emerged from the tunnel. Madrid lined up in the same way, with Thomas controlling the centre of midfield directly behind Figo. Beckham was to his right and Zidane was to his left, with Ronaldo up top with Raul. What a sight it must have been for the Ogre. It was like living a dream and by dictating the play to this group of household names, who were like his puppets, he was pulling their strings. This time, Madrid were in their away kit of all purple and were met with a familiar black and white onslaught from the home team, whose tails were up as they needed to score at least once inside the 90 minutes.

Thomas not only had the skills to compete but also had other things like the sort of brute strength and power that some superstars don't possess or develop. That was shown when Ibrahimović, who has a huge ego and never tires of talking himself up or grabbing any headlines he can, found himself isolated one on one with Thomas. The Swede used his deft touch to smartly slip the ball in between Thomas's legs — one of the cheekiest moves in football.

But if Ibrahimović thought that was the end of it, he was sadly mistaken. Thomas used his sheer power to get his body between Ibrahimović and the ball. The big striker is about six inches taller, but he couldn't do anything. Even with his long limbs, he squirmed around like an octopus, puffing out his cheeks, but helplessly watched the ball roll out for a Madrid goal kick. Maybe Ibrahimović had done the flash thing and earned a few screams from Juve diehards, but Thomas had won back possession, outsmarted him and shut down the attack. The Juventus pressure kept building like a tidal wave until on 75 minutes Trézéguet hooked a shot past Casillas to make it 1-0. Keen to hit back, Luxemburgo took off Beckham, Zidane and Raul but Thomas stayed on as he wasn't flagging and looked comfortable. Roberto Carlos hammered a free kick off the post and the score remained the same at 90 minutes. Half an hour of extra time ensued and then, with five minutes left and penalties looming, a mistake in the Madrid defence let Marcelo Zalayeta slot home. 2-1. That was it, Madrid crashed out and Thomas's Champions League adventure was over for the season. It had only lasted two games and one period of extra time, but he'd risen to the level and proved he could cut it.

It was not only some of his fans who thought that; the tough Spanish football media had now hopped on the Gravesen bandwagon. The newspaper *Marca,* which had mocked him up as Shrek, awarded him their maximum three-star rating for his performance in the home leg against Juventus and also in the following league game against Betis. Basically in just six weeks, Thomas had changed the perception of him from some sort of joke figure into a serious member of this celebrated team. They were appreciating his worth.

The fans in Madrid were now also embracing Thomas. One thing they'd noticed was during training when it was bitterly cold, quite a lot of the players would be wrapped up in gloves, tights, snoods and woollen hats to keep warm. But Thomas was out there, no hat, in his short sleeves and sprinting about like a man possessed. They were shocked to see one of their heroes training like a little boy. He really was living his dream and it was obvious to anyone who looked at him. It was thoroughly refreshing for a guy at his level to be showing it.

Danish tabloid *B.T.* dispatched a reporter whose full-time job was just to cover Thomas and shadow his every move. Danish football journalist Johan Lyngholm-Bjerge said, 'The interest from Danish journalists was massive. It was so huge having a Danish player at Real Madrid and he'd always be making jokes with Beckham, Zidane and the Brazilian Ronaldo. For us, it was like he wasn't a Galáctico, he was a happy schoolboy.'

Even Thomas's team-mates were stunned by his impact on the team. They might have been lauded by millions but they knew the game and they'd all had to prove themselves to get to where they were. They certainly realised what Thomas was capable of. Among those who benefitted the most was Beckham as with Thomas patrolling the centre of the pitch and feeding incisive passes to him, he could get forward and swing over his signature crosses, which were a defender's nightmare due to their speed and curl. That was the way Beckham had made his name in his Manchester United days, when he had Roy Keane looking after the central area. He gave the whole team a structure and a platform for Beckham and the likes of Ryan Giggs to go forward. Beckham, who was also England captain at the time, wasn't shy to admit the effect Thomas had. Becks said, 'He's a very strong player. I know it because in England, when we fought for the ball during games, I ended up with bruises and marks. Gravesen's arrival gives me the best of both worlds. I like playing out on the right and in the middle. If the two of us are together in the middle, it will give me more opportunity to try and get forward, which I haven't been able to do since I came here, and is something I love to do.' Fellow midfielder Borja Fernández echoed those sentiments, adding, 'Thomas played his role perfectly.'

For football fanatic Thomas, it was a dream start to his career in the big time. 'When a game kicks off at the Bernabéu and all the fans applaud, I just look at the crowd,' he confessed. 'I look at them and still can't quite believe that I am here.'

While he was 'the happy schoolboy', Thomas was still Thomas. Pictures began circulating around the globe of this off-the-wall Danish guy grabbing, grappling and throwing football's superstars around. It was something he'd always loved doing to team-mates and club staff, but Los Galácticos at Real Madrid weren't used to it. There's a great picture of Ronaldo being hoisted into the air by Thomas who's got hold of his shorts and training top. Another shows Roberto Carlos tumbling to the ground after Thomas had shoved him. Then there was his speciality, grabbing Solari and lifting him in the air, as his feet dangle around Thomas's knees. It didn't matter who they were, Thomas was still his old self. He wasn't putting on a persona no matter where he was.

There were reports that Thomas had also resurrected one of his old pranks of teabagging, which involved him pulling out his scrotum and trying to place it on an unsuspecting victim's head. It was a universe away from the usual goings-on at Real, where players were more in the news for dating models, buying ridiculously expensive pieces of jewellery or splashing out on a private jet to go to New York for shopping trips. He was one of Los Galácticos on the pitch, but not off it.

The next big hurdle for Thomas was to make his bow in the greatest club game of them all, El Clásico: Real Madrid against Barcelona. Not only are they the country's two best teams but they normally have squads full of globally renowned players. There is also a political element, with Madrid representing Spanish nationalism and Barcelona spearheading Catalan independence and the region's identity. This mix of politics in football isn't unique, but few games, if any, provide the electricity and tension of El Clásico. It's such a fierce battle that it's beamed around the world, and even non-viewers of Spanish football will usually make a point of tuning in.

Thomas got his first taste of it as Barcelona travelled to the Bernabéu. Madrid were behind in the league table and needed a win to keep their slim hopes of becoming champions alive. Regardless of league positions, every game between the two is a do-or-die affair, with no quarter given. We've already covered just how glamorous Madrid's squad was and they only just pipped Barcelona in that regard. The visitors arrived with one that almost matched it including Xavi, Andrés Iniesta, Samuel Eto'o, Carles Puyol and Brazilian genius Ronaldinho. You couldn't have pitted two teams of higher quality against each other; both were stacked with talent.

Zidane got the home team off to a perfect start by scoring after seven minutes. Ronaldo added a second before Eto'o pulled one back. Raul then scored, followed by Owen, before Ronaldinho got in on the act. After 90 minutes that flashed by, the final score was 4-2. It was a superb match, watched by many millions, and Thomas seemed to do no wrong. The victory was in the middle of another seven-game winning run, although Real failed again at the eighth attempt when Sevilla held them to a 2-2 draw.

Thomas ended up making 20 appearances for Real that season, which made him pretty much an ever-present after his shock transfer. One thing he did notice was that more bookings were coming his way. Traditionally, English football is rougher than the continental game, where physical play is not as tolerated. He said, 'When you look at some of the yellow cards I've had this year, I've only been given them because I'm so big compared to some of the other guys. Some of the cards, some of the sliding tackles, would have been applauded in England, but here I've been booked because of the rolling and the actors' classes they give. I will get used to it, but I won't take it out of my game the fact that somebody's going to get crunched. And I won't learn to dive: I'll be standing up as soon as I can. I have a picture of Duncan Ferguson breaking his arm and carrying on. He didn't go down; he got up, walked to the sideline and got substituted. I learnt from him that you don't lie down.'

Madrid finished the season strongly with a 3-1 win away to Real Zaragoza. Thomas had the right to go into the summer break with a great deal of satisfaction. He'd come to the world's biggest team and, with almost everyone writing him off, held his own with Los Galácticos and become a hero to the notoriously hard-to-please Real fans. His full-blooded attitude and maverick way of doing things was like nothing they'd ever encountered.

He'd ascended to the top of football's Everest and had every right to revel in it and take a minute to imbibe the sweet tonic of success.

What Thomas and the fans who adored him didn't know was that this idyllic situation was about to go up like a bonfire. Thomas, aged 29 and at his peak at Real Madrid, had fewer than 75 games left in his career.

Mad Dog was about to come off the tracks forever.

Chapter 15

Porn Cocktail

THOMAS'S downfall was caused by a cocktail of elements and influences that hit him hard. I don't think he even saw them coming. While he'd been able to stay focused during his first six months in Madrid, once the season stopped and he had a chance to survey the scenery, it dawned on him just how much attention was on him. The spotlight was burning brightly. Fans in Spain adored him and he was the biggest thing in Denmark.

The likes of Beckham and Ronaldo were accustomed to intense scrutiny of their lives, on and off the pitch. They'd never known any different since becoming footballers. They were well used to having paparazzi following their car or leaping out in front of them as they left a shop. Thomas had been able to live a fairly normal life in Liverpool and Hamburg. He'd been well known but never one to trouble the non-sports media regularly. That was no longer the case. He wasn't only big news in Denmark, he was fodder for every news outlet under the sun as being a Real Madrid star meant you were fair game.

Danish football journalist Johan Lyngholm-Bjerge explained, 'Even now, after he's retired, if something happens with Gravesen, it's all over the newspapers in Denmark as people love to read it. He doesn't feel he owes the media anything, as there have been clashes. He's had relationships with women and you can imagine if a famous football player starts a new relationship, it's all over the magazines and lots of the stories were probably not true. He got tired of that.'

Enter Kira Eggers, who politely declined to be interviewed for this book. She had been described as a 'porn star' and there's numerous X-rated videos featuring her online. She has also worked for Playboy TV and done raunchy modelling shoots. It soon broke that her and Thomas had become a couple. As if the interest in him wasn't already at fever pitch, getting together with a porn star sent Thomas's profile rocketing into a different stratosphere. It was the sort of story that tabloid journalists salivate about in their sleep. Thomas was in his first public relationship since parting with teenage sweetheart Gitte, and it couldn't have been more different. He'd gone from someone he'd known since his teenage days to someone who was used to attention in a completely different way. Unusually, someone within his personal circle actually broke ranks. Gitte gave an interview in which she expressed her surprise about his new partner.

Gitte said: 'Thomas and I had a very quiet life, and so I was very surprised to see him with Kira. I'm not so sure that Thomas takes the relationship as seriously as Kira. But I wish them both good luck. I am not jealous. We had our time together and have both moved on.' Not only that, she then revealed details about their relationship, which began after Thomas met a 15-year-old Gitte in Vejle. She revealed how Thomas was too shy to ask for her number, so enlisted a friend. Gitte added, 'I simply could not believe that the hard football player was too shy to ask me. So I let him sweat a little before I gave it to him and we immediately clicked and did all the things that normal young people do when they date.' Even a seemingly innocuous disclosure such as this would not have gone down well with Thomas, a notoriously private man who is very selective about who he speaks to.

With all this media interest fizzing around, things started to change drastically for Thomas. He was now being hounded by Spanish and foreign journalists, who wanted to know every detail of their famous footballers' lives. There was no escaping it. Not only was he under pressure off the pitch due to his romantic liaisons, but the niche he had carved out for himself on the pitch for Real was now in a state of flux too.

Florentino Pérez stuck religiously to his formula of buying a new superstar every summer, and so it was that Robinho became the latest to join the Los Galácticos ranks.

The pint-sized Brazilian, who was 21 and full of potential, left Santos — from the state of Sao Paulo — in exchange for €25m. His bamboozling dribbling skills, lightning-quick feet and flashy tricks had some hailing him as the greatest Brazilian since Ronaldo, who he was ironically joining in Spain. Arriving with Robinho was Spanish home-grown teenager Sergio Ramos, who moved from Sevilla and quickly became a legend. Even as I write this in 2018, he's still the main man in Madrid's defence and the club captain. These two had to play as they were part of the Los Galácticos mould, even if Luxemburgo didn't want to pick them. It was common knowledge at Madrid in those days that there was pressure from above. In addition, and more worryingly for Thomas, Real announced the arrival of midfielders Júlio Baptista and Pablo Garcia.

It was not going to be easy for Thomas to hang on to his place. Still in pre-season and even with the sprinkling of new players, Thomas kept his starting spot and in the first league game lined up in his usual centre midfield position as Madrid travelled to Cadiz. They won 2-1 with goals from Ronaldo and Raul. Maybe he hadn't been behind his signing but it was as plain as day that Luxemburgo wanted Thomas in the team. The pressure at Real is intense and there are no free lunches. If you were playing, it was because you could win matches. It will always be a club where being number one is paramount. No matter what you do, they want you to lift trophies.

What was also taking people aback was the fact that Thomas still had complete tunnel vision and belief in what he was doing. He would gesture to Zidane — regarded as the most ethereal footballer of all time – and order the big Frenchman around the pitch, almost saying to him. 'Look lad, I'll keep you right, follow my lead.' He had no inhibitions in shouting furiously at any of Los Galácticos. Thomas still had that stubborn drive to try to influence games as much as he could, even though it went overboard at times. But it seemed to be working, Thomas was fitting in and was now one of the lads. He kept his place for the second game of the season but Madrid lost 3-2 at home to Celta Vigo.

The new season meant Thomas would now also get a proper crack at the Champions League as Madrid were drawn in a group with Norwegians Rosenborg, Greeks Olympiacos and French champions Lyon, who they travelled to on the first matchday of the group. Being the start of the campaign, it was vital to get a win on the board to get off and running. The big teams tended to seal qualification early then rest players in anticipation of being busy come the season's end. So a full-strength team was selected by Luxemburgo with Thomas in midfield, but the Galáctico obsession of Madrid's hierarchy was causing havoc. Luxemburgo did his best but had to shoehorn them all in and upset the balance they'd ended the previous season with.

As the Champions League was then such a strong competition with no mugs, you couldn't field a team loaded only to attack. Lyon took full advantage and walloped Real 3-0.

In Madrid, losing two games in a row is a crisis. The newspapers are full of commentators, ex-players and fans speaking out, venting their disgust, ready to call for wholesale changes and whip up a frenzy of discontent. So Luxemburgo, feeling panicked, began to shuffle his pack in the hope of hitting on a winning formula that kept all the big-money signings happy. Thomas was benched for the next game at Espanyol, where they lost 1-0. Then, in the next Champions League game, he was a substitute again but came on late in the match as Real beat Olympiacos 2-1. The new guys were getting the starting spots now as pressure was being applied to make sure they were on the pitch.

Thomas was now out of the first-choice 11 but was coming on as sub, like he did in the next Champions League game against Rosenborg, which Real won 4-2. Then injury struck in the shape of a knee problem that would keep Mad Dog out of the first-team picture. He'd have to get fit again before he could even attempt to reclaim his starting spot.

As his rehab was ongoing, the Danish media discovered that Kira was planning her first trip to Madrid to watch Real play, even though a debilitated Thomas would be sitting in the stands with her. Journalists had been furiously digging around to find out anything they could and discovered the small detail that the couple had met in a Copenhagen nightclub. It was hardly Watergate but such was the appetite for information about Thomas's life that it made the papers. The revelation was treated as if it was some sort of major exposé, but it showed the media currency that Thomas represented.

Not playing football and with such intense focus on his private life, anyone who knew him could tell this was not what Thomas wanted. In fact, he would have hated it. He was a happy, bubbly guy who wanted to play football for hours every day and then be left alone as he followed a routine that suited him. Now, his career was in a serious jam and to put the tin lid on it, the only light at the end of the tunnel was an oncoming train.

While the team's patchy form might have been enough to keep them going in European competition, it was seriously hampering them in La Liga. With Barcelona storming ahead as they went into December, Florentino Pérez pulled the trigger as he couldn't countenance another season without the league title coming to the Bernabéu. He sacked Luxemburgo, who followed a long line of managers who'd tasted unemployment in the Spanish capital. If you weren't winning trophies, you were invariably on the verge of being axed as your job was on a knife edge without sustained success. Luxemburgo's replacement was Juan Ramón López Caro, who'd been promoted from the Real Madrid B team.

In his first game, the final clash of Madrid's Champions League group against Olympiacos, Thomas was in the starting line-up. Real lost 2-1 but they still qualified and could now focus on improving their league form, with the Champions League taking a break for a few months. Very little changed. Caro managed a win against Malaga, a home draw with Osasuna, a loss to Racing Santander and a goalless draw with Villarreal — a run that did very little to inspire fans or the club's directors. His appointment had a distinctly temporary feel to it. It appeared as if Caro was just keeping the seat warm until a big-name manager could be secured. The league already seemed lost and there was a good chance the new man was already being lined up, except that he was probably employed by another club so couldn't be announced until the season's end. With such a splendid squad, Real dug in and tried to pull things round. They went on a six-game winning run from between January and February 2006, with Caro coming to exactly the same conclusion as Luxemburgo: for the key matches, Thomas was well worthy of a starting spot.

So it came to the two games that would make or break Madrid's season. With the league way out of reach, they were drawn against Arsenal in the Champions League. The north London club were now in the second generation of Arsène Wenger's reign, with the likes of Cesc Fàbregas, Gilberto Silva, Kolo Toure, Mathieu Flamini and Alexander Hleb their main men. This was all Madrid had to play for; losing the tie would be a disaster and signal the start of their summer holidays, four months early. The first leg was at the Bernabéu and once again it saw Thomas up against

English opposition who would have been well aware of his strengths. It made a difference. Thierry Henry netted a superb individual effort to give Arsenal a 1-0 victory.

Two weeks later, Madrid found themselves in the last chance saloon at Highbury, Arsenal's home ground before their move to the Emirates in 2006. Thomas was again in the team as Caro seemed to select a side that mirrored the favoured Luxemburgo line-up. It was a war of attrition as Arsenal played with flair and freedom. Madrid looked tight and leggy because they knew how high the stakes were and what the reaction would be if they failed. Thomas's display epitomised that; he was out of sorts, got booked and was substituted with 20 minutes to go. It stayed goalless and Madrid crashed out, their season over. The players knew it. The fans knew it. Everyone knew it.

Now only one game mattered, their second league match of the season against arch-rivals Barcelona. It was the only chance they had left to save face and restore pride. It came in April at the Catalans' cavernous Nou Camp. Real were playing to rescue their dignity, to prove to the watching world and themselves that they could compete, and that this season had just been a one-off. Thomas was on the bench again in what had been a topsy-turvy season for him. He'd been in the team, then back out, then back in. As if to show how high the stakes were, the experienced Roberto Carlos got caught in the storm, received two quick bookings and ended up being sent off even before half-time. Zidane was then taken off and replaced by Thomas, and it was to be his last meaningful act in Madrid's famous white shirt. The game finished 1-1, rampant Barcelona were 11 points clear and summer couldn't come quickly enough for Real's scarred stars, who could at least draw some consolation from the upcoming World Cup in Germany. Well, for most of them that was, apart from Thomas.

Chapter 16

La Gravesinha

WORLD Cup 2006 would have been Thomas's fourth international tournament in a row, but the party went on without him. Denmark failed to book their place. They floundered in a competitive group that also included Kazakhstan, Georgia, Albania, Greece, Turkey and Ukraine. It wasn't that they lacked quality but it had been somewhat of a golden generation for the Danes. Despite some impressive displays over the past decade, getting to the World Cup finals wasn't a given for the country of fewer than six million people.

Whilst strong in Copenhagen, on the road the players didn't seem as able to rally and dominate games as they had before. Maybe age caught up. Europe's smaller nations had improved as they invested in infrastructure and saw their players gain experience in bigger leagues. The Danes lost twice — not a disgrace but it was their downfall — as

Ukraine and Turkey snuck through with impressive records that included only one loss apiece.

Thomas's last game of the campaign was Denmark's 1-0 win over Greece. A crowd of 42,099 saw him run over to take a corner and swing in yet another of his gorgeous, tantalising deliveries that left the goalkeeper flapping furiously, and Michael Gravgaard headed home. It was the last meaningful contribution Thomas would make for his country.

As a proud Dane, he featured in all the friendly matches as Olsen blooded some new talent over that summer, looking to overhaul things for the next competitive campaign. His final two games at home came fittingly in smaller stadiums, where his football journey started: the compact Fionia Park in Odense and the Brondby Stadion, against Poland and Portugal respectively.

Thomas's next move was always hard to predict and known only to himself. And it was the same with his international career. For some reason, he began the journey to Euro 2008, lining up in the first game of the qualification group against Iceland in Reykjavik. But he was substituted in the 70th minute and that was it. He'd played his last game for Denmark.

It was vintage Thomas that he made his final appearance in the Laugardalsvollur, a stadium that resembled a university sports centre, considering he could have gone out at any of the far grander arenas he'd strolled about in. But he bowed out with 66 caps, five goals and a fan in Mike Tyson.

Thomas had worn the red and white kit with distinction for the final time. He said, 'I'm very grateful for all the time I've spent with the team and I want to thank all my team-mates, coach Morten Olsen, the Danish fans and everyone involved with the team. It's been an honour to represent Denmark.'

There wasn't only upheaval in his international sphere as, predictably, Real Madrid's head honchos had dismissed Caro. He'd done nothing to galvanise the team and in his place this time was a Galáctico manager who was on the same level as the Galáctico players. Step forward Fabio Capello, who'd already managed the team back in the 1996/97 season.

Not only was there a 'new man' in the hotseat but Madrid's playing staff also went through an overhaul. The great Zidane retired, Ronaldo was leaving for AC Milan and Baptista was about to be sent to Arsenal on loan, with José Antonio Reyes coming in the opposite direction. A fresh batch of Los Galácticos were then recruited in the hope they could help Madrid start winning silverware again. They included Fabio Cannavaro and Emerson, the Juventus pair who had followed their manager from Turin. Manchester United goal machine Ruud van Nistelrooy arrived to much fanfare. Capello also brought in two central midfielders, Fernando Gago from Argentinean giants Boca Juniors for €20m and Mahamadou Diarra from Lyon for €26m.

These two spelled immediate danger for Thomas as they'd be competing directly for his position. The other issue was that Capello was well known as a strict, schoolmaster type. For example, during this time in charge of England's national team, he banned players from having ketchup or butter. Players were not allowed to order room service, walk around in flip-flops and shorts, and were forbidden from using their mobile phones in public. Rigid is the perfect word to sum up Capello's style, which England's star defender Rio Ferdinand likened to a 'prison camp mentality'. Thomas was always going to struggle in that type of environment, where any form of expression was clamped down on.

It was also at this time that Thomas appeared to change. His demeanour and body language indicated that he wasn't as comfortable as he had been. He was no longer the 'happy schoolboy'. The difference in him had arguably been caused by the massive interest in his relationship with Kira Eggers, perhaps by not playing as much as he wanted to in Madrid, or maybe by Capello's authoritarian rules. It could even have been a combination of all three, but Thomas's applecart had been upset.

Still, Thomas had two years left on his deal. He was 30 years old and was certainly still able to make a contribution. The problems had nothing to do with his ability. Thomas, along with the rest of the squad, set off for his first training camp under Capello in Irdning, Austria. It was there that Thomas saw red and flushed his Real Madrid career down the toilet.

The incident happened as the squad were playing a practice match, with cameras and media on hand to gauge how the new management team's changes were taking effect. The ball went out to wonderkid Robinho and Thomas crunched in with a tackle. Some reports say it was a bad challenge but either way the Brazilian didn't like the attention and physical treatment one bit. He pushed back against Thomas, who totally forgot the 'three stones' mind trick he'd been taught back in Vejle, and mauled the slight, twinkle-toed forward. Panicked team-mates piled in to save Robinho from a certain beating, several of them holding and blocking Thomas. But none tried to restrain Robinho, who was clearly grateful to be rescued from Mad Dog. The Brazilian walked away and made a 'crazy' gesture against his head, suggesting that Thomas had a screw loose while Thomas was snarling and pacing about the pitch like a caged tiger. Not only was Capello furious about the lack of discipline, but the world's media had once again caught it. One of the players present that day, Borja Fernández, said the fall-out it generated was not justified. 'There is always friction, it is a contact sport; sometimes you get angry and things happen,' he said.

It made headlines across the globe, partly because it was Real Madrid and partly because Robinho was seen as a future contender for the title of the world's greatest player. He was the Neymar of his generation. After the incident, when asked about Thomas, Capello rapped, 'His behaviour? I don't like it, he wants everyone to do what he wants, and I have told him so.' That sentiment echoed those of all the previous managers and players who'd encountered Thomas. But for all his success in winning five Italian leagues and a Spanish title in his first spell at Madrid, Capello's next statement showed he didn't really understand Thomas at all. 'I am not going to have problems with him,' Capello insisted. 'He is a little different but he works hard, which is important to me.'

No matter what Capello said, Thomas had burnt his bridges and was cut off from the group. Basically, he was in Siberia. Gago was handed his number 16 shirt and when the team flew to the USA for a money-spinning pre-season tour, there was no seat on the plane for Thomas.

It had been a dramatic deconstruction. He'd moved to Madrid after the best spell of his career, stayed focused and impressed enough to break into the starting line-up. He'd worked hard to gain the respect and praise of the Galácticos. Then he'd begun dating a porn star, seen his form dip, ended his international career, which had always been a source of solace and comfort to him, and was now being unceremoniously booted out by Real. Few players had seen their careers at the very pinnacle disintegrate so fast, and Thomas's, for some reasons of his own making, and some outwith his control, had folded like the proverbial house of cards.

But, 12 years on, Thomas is not thought of as the figure of fun in Madrid that some so-called experts proclaim in columns or on social media. An internet search for Real Madrid's worst signings will usually feature Thomas, described as a talentless hack who used to charge about the field like a headless chicken, kicking opponents or flying into reckless challenges. While it's certainly the case that he could lack tactical discipline and was a bruising opponent, Thomas fitted well into the Madrid team. His Galáctico team-mates said so in public and on the record, which they were under no pressure to do. On top of that, he'd cost a fraction of the normal transfer fee usually splashed out by Real. If Capello had been a bit shrewder with his man-management style and tried to make a connection with Thomas to understand his quirks, he could have utilised the undoubted ability the Dane possessed. But that never happened.

Lots of self-proclaimed football connoisseurs and hipster bloggers, who've never played the game at any serious level, have categorised Thomas as an overrated dud. The Madrid fans disagree; to them Thomas was and is a cult hero. One YouTube video dedicated to his time at the Bernabeu, entitled in Spanish 'We Will Never Forget You', has been viewed over five million times. Another written in English, called 'The Best of Thomas Gravesen', has close to half a million views. A further nine-minute film contains every touch he had in the El Clásico of April 2005. Anyone watching it would have to concede that Thomas looked a class act in what is still the biggest club match on the planet, featuring the dazzling superstars of Madrid and Barcelona. He showed that what all the football insiders had said about him was totally accurate — that on his day, Thomas was world class.

He also left Spain after making his Hollywood debut in the movie franchise *Goal!* The film tells the story of a fictional poverty-stricken youngster who dreams of becoming a football star and ends up signing for Real. Thomas plays himself, along with Beckham, Ronaldo, Robinho and Zidane, plus a host of other big-name players who make cameo appearances. Thomas's most memorable scene is when he's in an elevator with the film's protagonist, Santiago Muñez, as they're going back to their rooms in bathrobes and towels following a trip to the spa. Thomas and an accomplice stop the lift, yank away Santiago's towel and shove him out on to the landing in nothing but his birthday suit. Talk about art imitating life.

But the greatest legacy Thomas left in his wake at Madrid was his very own signature move. There aren't too many of them in the game, even among the bona fide superstars. Dutch wizard Johan Cruyff created his in the 1970s with his distinctive twist and change of direction, which became known as the Cruyff turn. Ronaldinho has his Elastico, where he flip-flaps the ball one way then the other in the blink of an eye, as if it's attached to his foot. Mexican magician Blanco had his Cuauhtemiña, where he'd grab the ball between both feet and then leap up over tackles. Perhaps the most famous is Antonín Panenka's self-titled penalty, where the player faked to smash it wildly before delicately dinking it down the middle, much to the frustration of the keeper, who usually dived one way expecting a powerfully blasted effort.

La Gravesinha was christened by fans during Real's home clash with Sevilla. The ball came to him and as he went to pass it, he misjudged it. So Thomas slid along the turf, put one knee on the ground, bounced back up in perfect time with the ball and ran on to it. At first look, it's a bit like watching someone on the street who trips and looks quizzically at the ground, as if refusing to admit they've just been clumsy and need something to blame. But watch it again and you notice that Thomas takes an opponent completely out of the game. He falls for his downward movement, allowing Thomas to run past him with the ball. At all times, Thomas is in perfect sync with the ball.

With a guy like Thomas, we'll never know. He was the sort of off-the-cuff natural footballer who could decide to do that in a split second. Football was one area where he was an undoubted master and could let instinct take over.

La Gravesinha — ironic joke or divine talent?

Chapter 17

Tartan Tommy

WITH his Real Madrid career over, Thomas had to find a new home to ply his trade. He was in the newspapers and linked with clubs all over Europe, as the move to Spain had afforded him a much bigger profile. One was Manchester United, whose manager at the time, Sir Alex Ferguson, reportedly saw Thomas as an ideal replacement for their now-departed midfield general Roy Keane. Fellow English team Newcastle United also showed an interest, along with their North East neighbours Middlesbrough. Former Barcelona and Tottenham Hotspur manager Terry Venables wrote in his newspaper column that Everton should make a move to resign Thomas. Madrid weren't going to be difficult to deal with as Capello had decided there was no future at the club for him.

This was the first time that Thomas had been involved in the sort of transfer saga that's rife in modern football.

Clubs are linked with numerous players but only ever sign a fraction. A rumour started to circulate that Scottish champions Celtic were keen on Thomas and in August 2006, he signed a three-year deal to go to Parkhead after a £2 million fee was agreed with Real. There were some last-minute details to be ironed out regarding Thomas's wages and some concerns about his knee, but they were all resolved. Newspaper reports pegged Thomas's earnings at £40,000 a week, a massive sum in the Scottish league which is nowhere near the commercial level of England or Spain. Journalists also wrote that his deal came with a £1 million loyalty bonus should he complete the contract. If the sums are accurate, Thomas would have easily been Scotland's highest-paid player at that time.

It was an exciting time to join the Glasgow club. They'd lifted the league title the previous season and were managed by motormouth former Scotland international Gordon Strachan. He'd had a distinguished playing career, most notably at Aberdeen and Manchester United, before working in the dugout. Inside the game, Strachan's still a Marmite character, either loved or hated. Never short of a word, he's known for his cutting comments during interviews and for often being a tricky customer to deal with. One of his most infamous exchanges went thus — Reporter, 'Gordon, can we have a quick word, please?' to which he replied, 'Velocity' and walked away. In another, he was asked about a difficult team selection and retorted, 'I've got more important things to think about. I've got a yoghurt to finish by today; the expiry date is today.' On the face of it, he looked like he might be a good fit for Thomas. Here was a manager with a bit of personality who might see a kindred spirit in his new highly paid midfielder.

It was also boom time for the Scottish league as Celtic's cross-city rivals Rangers had just taken on a new manager. The much-respected Frenchman Paul Le Guen had done some great work with Lyon and turned them into a force across Europe. Celtic had invested heavily to meet the domestic challenge head on, and on top of that also had ambitions of succeeding in that season's Champions League. Along with Thomas, Dutch striker Jan Vennegoor of Hesselink arrived for £3.4 million and midfielder Jiří Jarošík left Chelsea to come to Glasgow. Some Scottish steel was also added in the shape of Kenny Miller, Gary Caldwell and Derek Riordan.

With a host of new players, Celtic's fans expected success. Although they were nowhere near as big a club as Real, the fans demand results nonetheless. While Scotland is of similar size to Denmark, its two Glasgow clubs are outliers. They attract around 50,000 to 60,000 for home games when their teams are playing well. They are big fish in a very small pond. Thomas may have stepped away from the pressure cooker in Madrid and the glare of the world's media, but Glasgow wasn't a comfortable retirement devoid of pressure. Far from it.

Demands at Celtic are high. The team, along with Rangers, dominate their domestic league with ease. A couple of defeats can induce cries of panic. The pressure on the players is unrelenting and it's why some love to play for Celtic or Rangers, known collectively as the Old Firm. Some players simply can't hack it. Every move is scrutinised and football is like a religion in the city; it can be suffocating, as well as intoxicating, as nothing else dominates like it. Thomas had not been the major star in Madrid and could somewhat shelter in the shadow of Beckham and Zidane. At Celtic, he wouldn't have that luxury. He would be one of the focal points as not only was he earning the most, he came with the Galáctico tag. Very few first-team players left Real for a relative minnow league like Scotland's.

Just as he'd been the most written- and talked-about Danish player of his generation, Thomas was now about to get the same treatment in Scotland, where footballers are the only genuine celebrities. The country's TV scene is very small and most of its well known musicians move away. As if to underline the point, Scotland's biggest selling newspaper, *The Scottish Sun*, decided they had a classic tabloid story on their hands when sources confirmed that Kira was coming to Glasgow with Thomas. Even though their relationship wasn't new, the paper ran a front-page exposé, with a picture of a bikini-clad Kira alongside the headline 'Gravesen's Porn Star Lover'.

At that point, Thomas shut himself away from the media and in fact never gave another interview again during his career. He simply stopped interacting with the press and TV reporters altogether. He'd had enough and the probing into his private life in particular didn't sit well with him. His friend, Niclas Jensen, spoke of the toll the intrusion took on Thomas, revealing, 'Thomas did not feel he could be allowed to be himself. He is uncomplicated, honest and straightforward in many ways. He feels he has experienced that he could not be who he would like to be in public. He could not navigate it. Therefore he had the need to boycott the press when he did it.' Morten Olsen, his manager with Denmark's national team, who had always been able to get the best out of Thomas, agreed. 'I am not surprised that he chose to pull the plug to the public completely,' Olsen said. 'I think he needed it.'

Thomas posed for the cameras as he was unveiled by Celtic, looking fit and strong, and holding up the club's iconic green and white hooped shirt. He wasn't smiling; in fact he was deadpan. The fans didn't know it, his team-mates didn't know it and perhaps most people close to him didn't know it, but Thomas was damaged goods. Not in a football sense, but mentally; he'd been ground down by everything else going on. He was a sensitive soul who was not built for the modern-day adulation of footballers. Sadly, his love affair with the great game was on borrowed time.

That didn't mean he was withdrawn or sullen. In fact, during his time at Celtic, his maverick ways went into overdrive. The team's dressing room was full of international players and big characters like Polish goalkeeper Artur Boruc and tough midfielder, club captain Neil Lennon. Even with a robust squad, Mad Dog immediately made his presence felt, as Celtic full-back Mark Wilson revealed. 'I would say he was a bit odd,' he admitted. 'I didn't know what to expect when he came in. I'd heard stories about him and I'd seen him for years in the Premier League with Everton and then at Real Madrid with that crazy look. I always thought maybe he'd come into the dressing room and it would be a bit of an act or the things I'd heard weren't true, but it was far from it. This guy came in and, honestly, he was a breath of fresh air. An absolute joker, he got on with everybody. What a thoroughly nice guy he was.'

One thing that made a big impression at Celtic was Thomas's trademark bear hug. 'He'd grab somebody from behind in a big bear hug and pretend to hump them — and I'm not joking,' said Wilson. 'He'd do it with players, physios, doctors, staff, coaches, it didn't matter who it was. He was that strong; he was a big kid who loved a pretend fight. It was hilarious, as long as you weren't on the receiving end, watching someone trying to wriggle out of it.'

Thomas's debut came in early September when Celtic played away at Aberdeen, a city in Scotland's North East. They won 1-0 and Thomas, keen to stamp his authority on the game, received a yellow card. It was an important match for him as it was a few days before Celtic's Champions League campaign kicked off. They'd been drawn in a tough group with Benfica, FC Copenhagen and Manchester United. It was a mouth-watering section, with Thomas set to play at club level back home in Denmark for the first time since leaving Vejle as a novice.

The first game saw Celtic take on Manchester United at their hallowed stadium Old Trafford — nicknamed the Theatre of Dreams — in front of 74,031 fans. It was a massive game made even bigger by the Battle of Britain element, due to the rivalry between Scotland and England as old enemies. It was a chance for Thomas to prove to everyone watching around Europe that he still had plenty to offer, and it was also an opportunity to show United boss Sir Alex Ferguson what he had missed out on.

Thomas played from the start as Celtic took a shock lead thanks to Vennegoor of Hesselink. The Scots were buoyed by that and grew in confidence. But Thomas wasn't swept along and looked off the pace, giving the ball away too often. Despite his lack of tactical discipline at times, he was never known for misplacing passes. The home side equalised and then went 2-1 ahead after Thomas was caught again with the ball, which allowed an ultimately deadly counter attack to develop. Celtic's Japanese star Shunsuke Nakamura then curled in a peach of a free kick to make it 2-2 at half-time before United fashioned a goal early in the second half, again after Thomas lost possession, and held on to win 3-2.

Thomas had shown some nice touches and a few of his barnstorming runs up the pitch, but he was to blame for the defeat. There was no denying it. With it only being his second game of the season, he was understandably off the pace due to a lack of competitive action. It was mentioned by some commentators as one reason for him performing below his usual standard. Sadly, it was only the beginning of what was about to come.

Celtic's fans were keen to see Thomas show the class they'd seen at Everton and in Spain, as after all he'd been part of Los Galácticos and that comes with expectation. Then, in true Thomas style, in the most important game of Celtic's season against their Old Firm rivals Rangers, he stepped up to the plate. Almost 60,000 screaming Glaswegians packed into Celtic Park to see Thomas open the scoring. The ball was flighted across by skipper Neil Lennon and Thomas was running from midfield tracking it, only for winger Aiden McGeady to get there first. The goalkeeper palmed his effort out but Thomas dived to nod the ball into the goal. He flew over the line, along with the ball, and ended up tangled in the net. His relief was clear. For Thomas, he was proving he wasn't washed up; he was snarling and showing those infamous wild eyes. From then on, he became a cult hero for the fourth time at a different club. He was showing the fans how much it meant to him, to inflict damage on their bitter city rivals. Celtic scored again to seal a 2-0 win.

The squad had also realised that Thomas had bags of ability that seemed innate after seeing him at close quarters. Wilson said, 'When he went on the pitch, he was an outstanding player; almost when he wanted to, he could turn it on instantly. He had everything and that's what surprised me, coming from Real Madrid and all those great, skilful Galáctico players. He just got painted as the ball-winner who would give it to them but when he came to us, his skills were unbelievable. The tricks he could do in training, his technique, shooting, dribbling — he was a top, top player.'

Next up were FC Copenhagen, with Thomas facing his own countrymen in Glasgow. The game was decided by a penalty converted by Kenny Miller, but it was clear how much the victory meant to Thomas. He grabbed his team-mate in celebration, again with eyes wild and face contorted.

Then, on 12 November, Thomas ticked off another career first. Celtic were away to St Mirren in a league match at their Love Street stadium. Early on, the ball was crossed over and it broke in the penalty box to Thomas, who thundered it home with his left foot. Later in the game, he controlled a pass whilst turning and started running, dribbled past four jelly-legged defenders and smashed the ball in with his right foot. In the second half, Celtic got a corner that was whipped in to the near post, to where Thomas made a darting run and flashed it across the helpless keeper. A perfect hat-trick (his first and only) — left, right and head. On form and feeling comfortable, Thomas was way above Scottish league level and it showed in that game.

Later that month, Thomas took his place in the Celtic team that scored a famous win over Manchester United, which is still celebrated today. It was an engrossing Champions League tie, only decided when Nakamura hammered in a mouth-watering free kick from 30 yards as the green half of Glasgow went wild. The final fixture of the group stage saw Thomas back in Denmark, where he was a hero, for his last ever professional game there. Celtic were blitzed 3-1 by FC Copenhagen and it turned into a night Thomas wanted to forget. The silver lining was that Celtic had won all three home games and they marched into the last 16 to face AC Milan. While this was the bare minimum at Real Madrid, for a team like Celtic in one of Europe's minnow leagues and operating with very limited cash resources, it was almost like winning the tournament itself. The club had a good vibe about it but Thomas still seemed anguished.

It became an open secret that Strachan was finding it tough to deal with Thomas's headstrong manner. Whispers slipped out that Strachan didn't like Thomas's unique ways.

Quite simply, the manager — who would go on to manage the Scottish national team's unsuccessful bid to qualify for the 2018 World Cup – either couldn't or didn't want to make it work with his star player. Strachan kept trying to fit Thomas into a rigid system that had been proven to work at his other clubs. But it was the one thing Thomas could never align with. It was like asking a master painter to fix the electrics in your house. Team-mate Aiden McGeady lifted the lid on some of the goings-on. 'Strachan hated him, they didn't see eye to eye,' he said. 'I remember one time

Strachan had finished a team talk, I looked over at Tommy and Tommy is sitting in the corner of the dressing room with a newspaper with the eyes cut out, looking through it.'

It appeared to come to a head as Celtic went to the south side of Glasgow to play Rangers. Again, passions were sky high, as they are every time the two teams lock horns. Part of their intense rivalry stems from Celtic being a Catholic team and Rangers a Protestant one, and the fallout from historic clashes between the religions. During the team talk, Strachan read the riot act and implored Thomas to stay disciplined and not talk to the referee. He was ordered not to get involved in any verbal exchanges with the ref as he was collecting too many bookings, which could risk a sending-off and leave the team a man short. Then, by chance, the referee knocked on the dressing room door for the usual pre-match briefing and Thomas happened to be changing at the peg right next to the door. Thomas opened it, saw the referee and said, 'Sorry lad, I can't talk to you today.' He then promptly slammed the door shut in the referee's face.

Rangers captain Barry Ferguson also had a perplexing encounter with Thomas during the game itself as both teams were trooping off at half-time. Thomas thought it would be a good idea to find out more about his new city from a born-and-bred Rangers fan. Whilst the rest of the players were turning their minds to what was going to be said in the dressing rooms and what changes they could make to their own game, Thomas asked Ferguson if he knew of any good restaurants in Glasgow. He was met with a stunned look. Remember this was during one of the most bitter fixtures anywhere in the world, in a white-hot atmosphere, and here was Thomas badgering the opposition's skipper and main man for recommendations about where to get a tasty meal.

Even during the match, he was in maverick form. Thomas became an even bigger hero by again scoring against Celtic's bitter rivals, meaning he'd done it home and away. His goal this time was a gem; the ball was bouncing and spinning high, but he angled his body over it and lashed it into the net from an acute angle. It was a difficult skill that Thomas made look easy, as he normally did. It wasn't all plain sailing as Thomas was revelling in the fast-paced game and reacting to it, to the detriment of the rigid system that Strachan had insisted on. Wilson explained: 'We played at Ibrox and he scored a great goal; he was playing in midfield just ahead of me. It was the second half and Rangers were really coming on top of us and I'm saying to him, "Shut your right off Tommy." He just cracked and turned around, "Shut up lad, shut up." I thought he was joking, so five minutes later I said to him, "Shut your left off Tommy." Then he just turned around and shouted, "Shut the fuck up, lad, do not talk to me for the full game." That day, he played his own game; he didn't play a position, he would take off and didn't give a shit. He was supposed to be right midfield and he was everywhere.'

Other things about Thomas started to become clear. The Celtic players realised how intense he was and how he'd get fixated with things. Wilson said, 'He loved his pool; he'd come into training with his own cue ready to play. We'd be preparing for big games but he'd always have the cue, and go up after training to play. Sometimes he'd just play himself, he loved it that much. The youth players loved him and, to be fair, he knew all the young kids' names, probably more than I did. Thomas was the kind of guy who would stop in the street and chat to fans without any hesitation.'

Another thing he had no hesitation in doing was driving like a maniac. For some reason, Thomas didn't feel the need to wait in traffic. Celtic's stadium is located in the East End of Glasgow, not far from the city centre and in a fairly busy residential area. After games, it is usually gridlocked as the 60,000 fans try to disperse in a variety of ways using the same roads. While his fellow players would wait patiently in the jams reflecting on their performance, Thomas would drive his Honda car, provided to him free by the club, on the wrong side of the road. He'd accelerate hard all the way into oncoming traffic with his index finger held aloft out of the window. The gesture was supposed to be some kind of explanation to anyone wondering what was going on, but the finger seemed to confuse people more than explain anything.

Thomas had also tried to convince McGeady to join him in buying a shared car. By this point, despite being a multi-millionaire, Thomas had reined in any spending and was going through a period of conserving cash, for no apparent reason. Anyway, both of them lived in the exclusive

Thortonhall village, south of Glasgow. It's an area popular among footballers and well-off individuals. Thomas hit on the grand plan that he and McGeady should both contribute 50/50 towards the cost of a big Audi A8 4.2 diesel. The logical move for most people would have been for the two team-mates to share the driving, use their own cars and take it in turns to pick the other up. But for Thomas, the best idea was to buy a separate car together specifically for driving to training. He'd picked out the exact model; it wasn't a case of any car, it was *that* car. It illustrated again that his way of approaching situations was very precise, intense and focused. McGeady added: 'He thought differently to everyone else.'

By the turn of the year, Strachan had become tired of Thomas's antics and began leaving him on the bench. Sometimes he didn't even come on at all. He'd play in some games but wasn't the automatic pick he'd been when he arrived to much fanfare. One squad member, Derek Riordan, recalled how when Strachan barked out instructions on the training pitch, Thomas would stand behind him doing the universal chatterbox gesture with his hands.

His Celtic career had begun to seriously unravel by the time the Champions League knockout stages came round. Celtic lined up against AC Milan in the round of 16, with the first leg played at a packed Celtic Park. Thomas was dropped and Dutchman Evander Sno, who had a fraction of his talent but would stick to a rigid system, was picked instead. Thomas came on for the final nine minutes of a tense 0-0 draw. The second leg in the imposing San Siro stadium was a similar story as Sno started again in central midfield. Thomas entered the fray after an hour but couldn't impose himself as Milan won 1-0 in extra time thanks to a goal from the mercurial Brazilian Kaká.

Thomas's time at Celtic was nearly up. The team were playing well and romped home to win the league in style. One reason was that the Rangers manager Le Guen had horribly misjudged the Scottish league and ended up signing a lot of players who weren't up to it. That allowed Celtic to gallop away with the title, becoming champions by a 12-point margin.

Thomas's last game of the season was at Easter Road, home of one of Edinburgh's teams, Hibernian, and Celtic lost 2-1. Ironically, his midfield opponent that summer's day was Scott Brown, who'd agreed to join Celtic for £4.4 million the following season. At time of writing in 2018, Brown had played over 300 games for Celtic and is the long-term team captain, but it's hard not to think what could have happened if Thomas had been embraced by Strachan in the same way. The manager liked Brown and seemingly took a shine him, but as a pure footballer Thomas was in a totally different class way beyond Brown, who has never played outside Scotland.

For some reason it appeared to some fans and commentators that Strachan seemed to have an agenda and was keen to make it clear to everyone. Strachan wanted to ensure Thomas was aware that he'd had enough of him. The showpiece game of the season rolled around, the Scottish Cup Final at the national stadium, Hampden Park. Celtic were up against Dunfermline and bidding to do the league and cup double. It wasn't a classic game by any stretch of the imagination, with on-loan defender Jean-Joël Perrier-Doumbé scoring the only goal to give Celtic their second trophy of the year.

But Thomas never saw a second of the action. He was reduced to taking pictures with kids on the pitch as he wasn't even included among the substitutes. Unknown 20-year-old Icelander Teddy Bjarnason was bizarrely named as a sub – and went on to make a single appearance for Celtic over an anonymous four-year spell.

It was ludicrous to see a man who'd been able to command a place in the Real Madrid team less than two years earlier, at the highest level of the European game, being treated as if he couldn't perform in the far less demanding environs of Scotland — and then being publicly embarrassed. Here was a player who admittedly wasn't going to blindly follow instructions and often struggled to curb his eagerness, but had a level of football intelligence way in advance of the system he was part of but it seemed to some the manager didn't want to face that.

Mark Wilson added: 'He was a player who needed a free role. It's difficult to do that if the guy doesn't have ability, as then you're playing with a man down, but I felt Thomas had the ability to see a pass and score great goals. It wasn't that he didn't like working hard; his fitness levels were top notch.'

Thomas finished the season with 29 appearances and the only medal of his career, for winning the Scottish Premier League title in 2006/07. He never played competitively for Celtic again.

Chapter 18

Ferry Cross the Mersey (Again)

IT was a Groundhog Day nightmare for Thomas. He'd been informed for the second successive summer that he was *persona non grata*. First Real Madrid, now Celtic. His manager in Glasgow, Gordon Strachan, spoke about the decision to wield the axe and revealed that Thomas wasn't disruptive. He said, 'I spoke to Thomas and told him he won't play for us because of the system we play. We tried our best to get a system which suited Thomas and it hasn't worked. It was the system to blame, not the player or the club. Thomas finds it difficult to fit into our system and he'll tell you that himself. He'd rather play in a system that suits him and we can't change our style of play to suit one player.' While the manager's honesty had to be admired, it still begged the question why the club had made him the highest-paid player in Scotland on a three-year contract. His maverick ways were hardly a secret, but now he'd been kicked to the kerb because of them.

Thomas headed off for the summer holidays to get a break from the bleakness, as his love for the game seemed to be waning. He had the entire club scratching their heads about what his plans were. Normal service is for players to be pictured on golden beaches in far-flung places, cruising about in exotic sports cars or on Sunseeker yachts. After all, they're wealthy young men with free time on their hands, but not Thomas. Celtic team-mate Mark Wilson explained: 'When he came to the club, I was 23 or so, we were all into *Call of Duty* at that point, so when Thomas came in he said he played it as well. We didn't know how good he was and he said his mate was the top player in the world. We looked him up and he was. Then, at the end of that season, when we asked him, "What are doing in the summer?", Thomas said "Just back home, lad" and he said he'd go back to his parents' house, go in the basement and play computer games constantly. I'm thinking, "Jesus Christ, this guy has got millions, he could go anywhere in the world and at that time he had his porn star girlfriend. And he goes home to sit in a basement." It was so far from what a footballer of his stature was about.'

But it was precisely what Thomas would have lapped up. It was what he did every summer during his break from football. He adored being out of the spotlight. That's what he enjoyed and with his career in chaos, it would have been a welcome relief. When he returned to Glasgow, Thomas was still way out of the picture but an immediate transfer didn't look on the cards. He had to train with the youth team and to the surprise of many, he didn't sulk. In fact, he embraced it. Indeed, some of the players in that youth team have spoken about how focused and dedicated Thomas was. It didn't seem to matter to Thomas what level or what venue he played in; he just wanted to play the game he loved. With the pressure-cooker environments in the Real Madrid and Celtic first teams swallowing him up, he would have been glad just to be able to play. That's all he wanted to do.

One incident with the youngsters that is still talked about a lot saw Thomas playing in a practice match amongst the squad. His team were 3-0 down when Mad Dog snapped. He grabbed the ball and began shouting at the coach 'No lad, we start again, 0-0.' And they did. It was easier than arguing with a man who was cut from a different cloth than virtually everyone else in professional football. He would do this quite often if he didn't like the way the result was going.

Another quirk that didn't go down well with the Celtic bosses, but is still remembered by the players, is Thomas's famous 'don't shout at the shooter' rants. The outbursts happened when the players took part in practice matches in training. As is the norm at all levels of the game, from school children to top professionals, when you want the ball you shout for it. It's unheard of to play the game in silence and remember these guys are used to strutting their stuff in front of crowds of 60,000 or more. Shouting to help your team-mates in the game is an essential part of it. Thomas had played at some of the biggest stadiums on the planet and was no stranger to noisy cauldrons. Aiden McGeady remembers getting one of the now-infamous shooting blasts from Mad Dog. 'I remember one time when he was just about to shoot and I'm going, "Tommy, Tommy". His leg comes back, he stops the ball and is holding someone off and he goes to me, "Don't shout when I'm about to shoot, lad. I hate it, it's the worst thing in football, I hate it, lad. Don't ever shout at the shooter."'

This sort of quirky behaviour was making it even harder to see any way forward for Thomas. His chances of getting any game time in Glasgow were minimal, so he began to scout around for options. Sitting in the shadows with no chance of playing competitively would have been purgatory.

The issue is that public perception counts for a lot in football. If you're flying, playing well and scoring goals, it's easy convincing boards of directors to authorise spending millions on a player and meeting their wage demands. But when the player is at a club that don't want him, and is well paid with a big reputation to boot, it's a near-impossible sell. Warning signs flash, as any interested buyers ask, 'Why are they so desperate to get rid of him?' If you're a middle-of-the-road player, it's easier to get someone to take a chance as you can drop down into a lower league and rebuild. But for someone like Thomas, with his CV, a recent Galáctico and with massive earnings too, he was never going to attract a smaller club, even though he was more than good enough for them, in Britain or even Europe. It would have been too risky for a club with limited resources to take a chance on him. Lower-league teams go for tried and tested pros who specialise at that level.

Negotiations carried on behind the scenes and at the end of August 2007, Everton announced that they were bringing Thomas back to Goodison on a season-long loan. The rationale was pretty simple. Thomas had been their best player only three years earlier and they were getting his services without a transfer fee. It was also a good move for Thomas; he'd been in a state of flux since leaving Everton, so he was clearly keen to get back to the form and equilibrium he'd previously enjoyed. While contracts are confidential, it's likely that Everton were picking up his £40,000 wages, but with the vast amounts of money sloshing around English football that wouldn't have been a huge issue. It was also a chance for David Moyes, who was still going strong as Everton manager, to get Thomas back to doing what he did best. Moyes knew exactly what he was getting. Mad Dog had been a pivotal figure in his team before leaving for Real Madrid. After the shock deal was announced, Thomas said, 'I have always said I would never want to come back to any club in England other than Everton — I am an Everton player. In my five years here, we improved all the way and we ended on a high and that is what I want to achieve again.' He couldn't wear his old number 16 jersey as that now belonged to central defender Phil Jagielka, so Thomas was handed number ten.

It's hit or miss when players return to old clubs. Maradona lined up for Boca Juniors in 1981 as a devastating and exciting protégé before leaving for the vast riches of Barcelona a year later. After a 15-month ban for submitting a positive cocaine test, he came back in 1995 with many expecting him to lead the team to past glories. Instead, it was an unmitigated disaster. Having initially been classified as an unpaid coaching assistant due to the ban, Maradona played once his suspension ended before failing yet another drugs test. Similarly, in 2012, a young Paul Pogba left Manchester United for Juventus, frustrated that he was not getting a chance to showcase his ability in the first team at Old Trafford. After a superb four-year spell in Turin, he came back to United for £89 million — a world record transfer fee – in 2016. The same happened with a teenage Cesc Fàbregas, who walked out on Barcelona to join Arsenal and developed into one of Europe's best midfielders. The Spanish giants were so impressed that they forked out £35 million to bring him home.

Thomas wasn't coming with the same profile as those guys, mainly due to Celtic wanting to wash their hands of him and everyone knowing it. But it still remained an intriguing prospect to see if he could match his previous level, or even surpass it. Thomas's new spell began brightly as he made his second Everton debut away to Bolton at the Reebok Stadium. In a strange twist of fate, he came on as a substitute for his old midfield sidekick Lee Carsley with the game locked at 1-1. In the last minute, Everton were awarded a corner and Thomas went right back to his old job as if slipping into a pair of comfy old slippers. He delivered a sublime corner, just like all the others that had brought the team so many goals, and so it did this time as strapping defender Joleon Lescott climbed to power home. Cue Thomas, who went apoplectic as he celebrated with the Everton fans. Mad Dog was back with a bang. His manager David Moyes said, 'Thomas Gravesen made a massive difference to us when he came on. He brought a calmness to us and made us play better. He's lacking a bit of fitness but he made some killer passes that helped us win the game.'

That momentum was cruelly cut short after Thomas suffered a knee injury in training, which put him out of contention. He managed to get back into the squad by the end of October, but was an unused substitute in a league game against Derby County.

Thomas was on the bench and came on for 25 minutes as the Toffees beat Greek side Larissa 3-1 in the group stages of the UEFA Cup. Back on domestic duty, Thomas got a five-minute run-out during Everton's 3-1 victory over Birmingham City.

There was never any consistency. Moyes had a midfield that was working well, featuring Thomas's old team-mates Tim Cahill, Leon Osman and Lee Carsley, as well as others such as Spanish technician Mikel Arteta, experienced ex-Manchester United man Phil Neville and South African slickster Steven Pienaar. Thomas couldn't get any traction to nail down a permanent place. It was understandable that Moyes would stick with a team that were playing well, plus Thomas wasn't his player; he was on loan and, as such, a borrowed asset. It would have been naive to put the house on him, although there was likely a clause to make the loan permanent should Everton have wished.

Ironically, as if they'd travelled back in time with Thomas in the squad, Everton were once again up near the top of the league, just like they'd been during his stellar 2004/05 season before Real Madrid came calling. This time, they were in fourth with ten games left, but end-of-season jangling nerves resulted in stuttering performances and the team ended up in fifth. The loss of that one position meant they missed out on the Champions League but still qualified for the UEFA Cup. On its own, it was a great achievement for Everton given their relative financial position compared with their league rivals, but it was still disappointing after being so close to the Holy Grail of European football, the Champions League. It was bittersweet but the initial reaction would have been like a punch to the solar plexus.

The final game of the season was at Goodison and Newcastle United were the visitors on a fresh, sunny Sunday afternoon in May. The conditions were perfect, with the pitch like a bowling green, and also idyllic for fans to sit and enjoy the action. Both teams scored in the first half, Yakubu for Everton and Michael Owen — Thomas's former team-mate at Madrid — for Newcastle. Then in the second-half Lescott scored and Yakubu stroked home a penalty to make it 3-1, which was to be the score as the final whistle blew.

With 85 minutes on the clock, Thomas came on as a substitute, replacing the powerful young striker Victor Anichebe, for only his 13th appearance of the season. The 39,592 supporters watching on didn't know that they were witnessing the last meaningful act of Thomas's fascinating professional career.

That nondescript five-minute cameo was the final contribution from the last of football's mavericks, as he said goodbye to the professional game. He'd played most of his days with a smile, described by phrases like 'the happy schoolboy' and 'the big kid'. But now it was over.

Aged 32, despite being fit and still possessing incredible ability, Mad Dog was no longer barking. He'd fallen out of love with football and didn't seem comfortable in his own skin. He would never kick a ball again in earnest. But his story and days of making headlines weren't over, not by a long chalk.

Chapter 19

Curtains

EVERTON officially announced that they were not keeping Thomas on and dispatched him back over the border to Celtic, with manager David Moyes saying, 'Thomas Gravesen will depart following the completion of his season-long loan. He deserves thanks for both his spells here and we wish him well for the future.'

After heading home to his parents' basement for his annual summer holiday bonanza of video gaming in the darkness, Thomas returned to Glasgow. Celtic's first team went on a pre-season trip to Portugal but Gordon Strachan, who was still their manager, froze him out. There was no place on the plane for Thomas.

To Thomas's infinite credit, he didn't take it personally and throw his toys out of the pram but instead sought out Celtic's reserve team manager Willie McStay, to whom he made it clear he wanted to join them on their trip of Ireland.

It was testament to Thomas's character that he could have stayed in Glasgow, without having to do much. But here he was taking the initiative to go on a trip with novice professionals and play a bunch of part-timers.

The opposition was Donegal Celtic, who at time of writing had just been relegated from the Northern Ireland Football Premier Intermediate League. It couldn't have been further removed from Thomas's recent past facing Juventus and Barcelona in front of a global audience of millions. Here he was now facing taxi drivers and plumbers. The others on the trip were mainly young players who had failed to make a big impression at the top end of the game. Also present was Derek Riordan, another first-team player Strachan had judged surplus to requirements.

One of the youths, Simon Ferry, remembers the trip and Thomas being there. 'You'd have thought he was a 16-year-old kid; he was one of the boys,' Ferry said. 'On the way over to Ireland, he was talking about this new *Batman* movie. He was going up to boys single-handedly at a time, "If we get time off, you come see [sic] the *Batman* film with me, lad?" Then we got told we had a day off and we were going to see the new *Batman* film as Thomas has organised it. He's sitting on the bus and I've never seen him so happy. We get to the cinema, Thomas front row, middle seat, biggest box of popcorn, biggest drink ever. For the next three days, he pretended to be The Joker from the film, so if someone was getting angry in training, he'd be like, "Why so serious, lad?" This replaced another of Thomas's common phrases at training where he'd accost some of the younger players with, "If you're not happy lad, go work in Sainsbury's.'"

The only other action Thomas saw was 45 minutes in another warm-up against Manchester City. He'd been stripped of his dignity and left twisting in the wind publicly. He remained the highest-paid player in Scotland but wasn't deemed worthy of being around the team. When asked by reporters how he saw Thomas's future playing out, Strachan said, 'I'm not worried one way or the other how it pans out because he'll still get treated properly if he stays here.'

That seemed a bizarre statement to make. Firstly, with the amount of money tied up in Thomas and, secondly, for Thomas's own personal welfare. It seemed to suggest that Celtic had washed their hands of him. It's incredible to think how quickly a player of Thomas's class had fallen from playing in Real Madrid's starting 11 at the summit of the game.

If Thomas's treatment had been isolated, then maybe it could be inferred that Celtic that done all they could and were forced to take such drastic action. But the season before, a situation had developed with another of their big-earning players, Bobo Baldé. The hulking Guinean defender, who was 6ft 3in and weighed 14 stone, had been adopted as a hero by the fans for his crunching tackles and brute force. Bobo was the fulcrum of the defence that saw Celtic reach the 2003 UEFA Cup Final, losing to a then-unknown José Mourinho's

Porto. He'd been rewarded with an improved contract, which the media's inside sources claimed was worth £30,000 per week. He'd been a regular starter for the team until 2006. From then on, he only played 14 games over his final three seasons at Celtic. Reports began to emerge in the newspapers that he wouldn't fit into the team's dynamic and refused to take orders. This was despite him being an experienced player who'd proven himself beyond doubt, and had been awarded a lucrative contract. Does that sound familiar?

Big Bobo wasn't like Thomas, who deliberately stayed away from journalists, and didn't let things swirl around in public without answering back. In October 2007, Bobo said: 'I want to make it clear about the situation and the people who are talking rubbish about me. They think I am just here to pick up my money and not work hard, but I am working hard to be at my best. I have come back from a broken leg and pelvic injuries, so I am not just here to sit and pick up my money every week. I will leave the way I want and not how Peter [Lawwell, Celtic's chief executive] or other people want. I have been told that I am not in the top two defenders and that I am down to sixth on the list. The manager and Peter told me this. If you are not wanted, then you leave, but I have two years left on my contract and I will leave in the way that I want and when I want.' Bobo — one of 13 siblings from a family who'd emigrated to Marseille — stuck to his principles. His contract ran out and he left the club in the summer of 2009 as a free agent.

Granted, it was impossible to be privy to all the goings-on in the cases of both Thomas and Bobo, but there were definite similarities. Some believe Celtic's actions damaged their standing as a club that prides itself on its caring, inclusive image. When two respected professionals became surplus to their agenda, they made it crystal clear their futures lay elsewhere.

Thomas's situation didn't fester for as long as on 18 August 2008, his contract was terminated. As ever in dressing rooms, stories came out, including one that had Thomas leaving with a £1 million golden goodbye. In return, he'd forsaken the £2 million he was due for the final year of his contract. Per game, he'd cost Celtic approximately £264,000. Without doubt, both club and player had paid a fortune, in contrasting ways.

From then on, things went very quiet and dark for Thomas. There didn't seem to be rumours or newspaper talk about him interesting other clubs, which would have been expected. Clearly, he would have been able to get a deal somewhere else, as he was a free agent, so there was no need for a transfer fee. He could even afford to take less in wages due to his pay-off and previous earnings. Something just didn't add up. It was clear that any enquiries were being stonewalled by his camp, which was still led by 1980s star John Sivebæk.

Some media reports linked Thomas with a return to Vejle. Thomas surely would have seen that as part of his masterplan to go back to where it all started, just like his heroes Sivebæk, Allan Simonsen, Ulrik le Fevre and his mentor Ole Fritsen had done. It was the culture in Vejle: fly the nest, represent the small team and town with pride on the world stage and then come back to pass the baton on to the next generation. Thomas was a seemed perfect fit for that. He was the biggest football star and celebrity in Denmark, and he'd been right to the top of the game, the absolute pinnacle, at a time when it exploded commercially. Everyone in the country knew his name. Coming home would have seen him crowned the new king of Denmark. His family still lived in the area and Kira was also from Denmark. It seemed to be the most logical and natural move. Plus it would have suited his personality too; he could get back to just playing the game he loved without all the interferences and complications he'd encountered in his final years.

But Thomas marched only to the beat of his own drum. So after seven months in limbo, floating around and being without a club, Thomas finally announced that he was retiring with immediate effect. His statement read, 'I have had fantastic years abroad. I played and lived in four countries. There are many people I need to thank. I would do it all over again if I had the opportunity.' This was the most Thomas had spoken in public since 2006, when he decided to stop doing interviews and shut himself away.

And that was it. Thomas disappeared off the face of the earth. No one heard from him, he didn't have any social media accounts and he didn't pop up on sports shows or in newspapers. Thomas was off the radar to the extent that some people almost started to forget him and lock him away at the back of their minds.

It takes someone with a very unique character to be able to do what Thomas did in this day and age. Camera phones and insatiable 24-hour news coverage are the norm. Most people in the public eye want to advertise what they're up to for commercial reasons, and even the ones who don't usually end up being snared by opportunistic photographers and journalists, with or without their consent.

But Thomas was nowhere to be seen. There was nothing for the media, particularly the Danish contingent, to get their teeth into. That was apart from one reported reappearance at Celtic a year after he left, according to Simon Ferry. The situation is explained as follows: Simon and some of the younger players were walking up to the stadium to take their seats to watch a first-team game, when they caught sight of Thomas marching up behind them. He was decked out in the official club suit he'd clearly kept tucked away in his wardrobe and brought back out again. Simon said: 'He said, "You want a game of pool up in the players' room, lad?" The youngster declined the offer for fear of getting a rollocking from the manager or anyone else in the club's hierarchy.

It would be another four years before anyone heard about Thomas. Even those tales, which received global media coverage, were shrouded in mystery as none of them came from him and seemed to contain dubious facts.

He wouldn't speak on the record in public again until 2018. So what became of Galáctico Thomas Gravesen, the last of modern football's mavericks?

Chapter 20

Keyser Söze

THE next time Thomas surfaced was four years later. He hadn't been mentioned by anyone or appeared in any newspapers. He'd been a ghost.

When Thomas was finally tracked down in 2013, he was living in a lavish gated community in Las Vegas. Tennis power couple Andre Agassi and Steffi Graf, actor Nicolas Cage and superstar magician Penn Jillette were his neighbours.

Mad Dog had settled down in Sin City's suburb, Summerlin, which lies on the edge of the spectacular Spring Mountains. He was living in the luxurious Canyon Fairways, where houses sell for small fortunes and a price tag of $5.5 million and upwards is not rare.

This had been reported by Søren Hanghøj Kristensen, a journalist on Danish tabloid newspaper *B.T.*, and at the time of writing this book, Thomas's US-based company

Thomas Holdings LLC was still registered to that address in Vegas.

Thomas hadn't lost his love of speed and was regularly seen burning up the Nevada freeways in his Mercedes SLR McLaren. It had a top speed of 208mph and cost around $500,000. With the climate being sunny and hot, Thomas was happy driving a lovely car like that; there was no need for him to have a battered Nissan Micra on standby for any gloomy winter weather. His Mercedes was so exclusive that only 2,157 were made worldwide and each one could be individually crafted to the buyer's specifications. It's as bespoke as it gets in the car world and to be frank, it's precisely the type of machine you might imagine Thomas jumping into to do his groceries.

America is becoming a common destination for ageing European footballers, with Beckham, Zlatan Ibrahimović, Thierry Henry and Wayne Rooney all seeing out their twilight years there. Thomas hadn't gone for that. In fact, what he was doing in America has still not quite been determined. One definite aspect was that he was able to escape the spotlight that had come to blight him. He didn't have journalists following his every move and because football isn't a major sport in the US, the general public in Vegas didn't recognise him. One of his friends told me for this book that Thomas would walk around and no one would even give him a second look. It's a paradox, as most top professional athletes find losing the interest and limelight difficult to deal with. Not Thomas. He wanted to disappear and did so well in that endeavour that he was even described in an article by Kristensen as 'a unicorn', the most famous of all mythical creatures.

One thing that was clear was that Thomas was no longer dating porn star Kira Eggers. She has since changed career and now runs a successful fitness business as a nutritionist and personal trainer. Their break-up was announced close to the time he left Celtic as Kira put it on her blog. It wasn't a surprise to many. They seemed to have polar opposite attitudes to life.

When news broke of Thomas's new set-up in Vegas, it mainly revolved around his new partner Kamila Persse. She had posted pictures online of them together in each other's arms. Kamila reveals on social media accounts that she works as a real estate agent for Berkshire Hathaway, the multinational conglomerate whose CEO is the revered investor Warren Buffett, known as the Sage of Omaha, who in 2018 was named the third richest man in the world. She's originally from Frýdlant in the Czech Republic but is based in the US. There are also descriptions of her as a model, but they're hard to verify. Some reports say they got married, while other reports refer to Kamila as Thomas's girlfriend. There's also a child involved, who appears to be from Kamila's previous relationship.

It's frustrating to write a book on someone surrounded by so much speculation, and whose life is shrouded in mystery.

But it's also mightily refreshing. With other international footballers, it would be an arduous task to uncover anything that's not already on their Wikipedia page and would take less than 30 seconds to check if they were married. But that's part of Mad Dog's charm and why there's so much intrigue around him. Very little is actually known about his life; there are rumours and reports but virtually no confirmation. Thomas isn't easily accessible either and, of course, any attempts I made to speak to him for this book were rebuffed. I did reach out to Kamila, who graciously replied and didn't deny knowing him, but told me Thomas was back in Denmark and if I had any questions to contact his old agent.

What is known is that Thomas would return to Denmark twice a year. He has a penthouse apartment in Vejle, which he bought for 14 million Krone [£13 million] in a building known as The White Facet. It's a 17-storey complex and the tallest building in the town by a distance. Thomas's place has access to the roof terrace and there's also an underground car park, so he can come and go in relative secrecy. His main plan was to live in a stunning purpose-built house closer to where he's from at the Daugård Strand, which has a panoramic view over the breathtaking Vejle Fjord. It's only a few kilometres from where Thomas's family home was, so it would have seen him close to all his friends and family. The blueprint states that Thomas bought the 4,280 square metre plot of land for 10 million Krone and it housed an old farmhouse, which was due to be demolished.

That would have left Thomas with a blank slate to construct his dream home, which was reported to have a 25 million Krone budget. As was normal in the world of Thomas, the developers Bo Plan ApS refused to divulge any information on the project, which was naturally a big deal in that sleepy corner of Denmark. A spokesman said, 'I can confirm that we work for Thomas Gravesen. But we have promised not to say anything more about the project.'

Things hit the skids when Thomas was blocked after being refused a building permit to construct the villa. His advisers had assumed that there was a buyback clause that meant if the permit didn't materialise, the money would be returned to him. Unfortunately, the seller had since gone bankrupt, so he was stuck with the land and no legal recourse to use it. From what can be gleaned, Thomas still owns the land but nothing appears to be happening with it. It's a proverbial white elephant.

All of this leaked into the public arena due to revelations about Thomas's wealth. According to numerous reports, in Nevada he hadn't just lapped up the sun and amused himself. Out of nowhere, newspapers broke the story that Thomas had amassed a fortune of over £80 million, with some even saying it had hit £100 million. The story was also run by major outlets such as the BBC, the *Daily Mail*, *The Sun* and Eurosport. This is where Thomas's story gets really interesting as there are lots of theories about how he made that money. But none are clear-cut and neither can they actually be documented. Also, of course, there's no comment from Thomas to confirm or deny that he made that amount.

By a process of elimination, what do we know? He did move out and set himself up Vegas in a palatial home. I've spoken to people who've been there to visit him. Also, his ex-team-mate at Celtic, Mark Wilson, said, 'I went out to Vegas with my wife and I was walking past the pool at the MGM, and who do I hear shouting on me? I turn around and there's Thomas lying on a sun lounger. I went over and we were chatting, and I asked him, "So are you on holiday?" He said, "No lad, I live here." And I just thought to myself, "What a stupid question, of course you do."'

Another ex-Celtic team-mate met Thomas by chance in Vegas and confirmed that he was exactly the same one-off character even out of the limelight. Nothing had changed about his behaviour. Former central defender Stephen McManus was on a stag-do and came across Mad Dog. 'Thomas was doing the exact same thing. He had this thing about if we went for a night out, all of us would be drinking, whether it was bottles of Peroni or Budweiser. Thomas had this thing about holding his thumb over his drink. We're standing there and Thomas would take his thumb off, drink his beer quickly and put his thumb back on it. He'd say, "Somebody could spike my drink, lad." And in Vegas, he was doing the exact same thing at a pool party when I saw him.'

It's clear that Thomas was out in Las Vegas, but the conundrum remains: how had he made himself so rich?

The first theory was that he pumped his cash into running casinos and bars. Those fared well and delivered a generous return. But to earn the astronomical sums that Thomas has, it would have needed to have been some set of establishments to generate that sort of return. The stumbling block is that nothing can be found to tie him into owning any establishments, or even references to his involvement in any businesses.

The second story doing the rounds is that Thomas became so good at *Call of Duty* that he moved up the professional ranks and became the second best player in the world. He was well known to be a really avid player during his playing days, so the theory was that he used his free time to become world class. E-sports are big business, sometimes attracting bigger crowds than even some live sporting events. It's possible he could have made a lot of money winning tournaments and also bagged sizeable appearances fees for being a superstar of that world. I reached out to some well-regarded video game journalists, who said that this theory was completely untrue. There was nothing to connect Thomas with the professional gaming world, even if he did have a username to hide his true identity. The experts say it would definitely have leaked out. Ironically, his former manager at Celtic, Gordon Strachan, made this claim about Thomas being a *Call of Duty* pro in an interview available on YouTube.

The third suggestion is that Thomas swapped one sport for another and became a poker professional. On the Global

Poker Index, there's an article stating that Thomas signed up for the World Series of Poker (WSOP), where the first prize in 2018 was $8.8 million. There were media reports of Thomas announcing he was retiring from being a businessman and would see out his days playing poker for a living. He did play in the 2008 WSOP European event in London and seemed to fare well relative to the other players. The buy-in was £10,000, so while it was a good standard it wasn't a huge amount of money for Thomas considering what he is reported to have made.

But what *is* a huge amount of money is the tale that first appeared on poker forum Two Plus Two. The story goes that some poker insiders were in a Vegas casino and became engrossed in an electric high-rollers game, featuring Thomas. A post made by a user going under the name TarantulaGargantu read, 'I can confirm he has made 80 million but it did not come easy. I was there in one of the sessions where he was playing some guy heads-up and lost 54 million in one night. Can't say who it was against, though.' Heads-up means that it's one on one, instead of the usual group of players around the table, all competing against each another. As it's an American website, we can assume the staggering amount that Thomas is claimed to have lost is in US dollars. The identity of his opponent being kept secret only makes the suggestion more credible. It would have been easier to throw out a bogus name of someone famous and allow it to filter through to the gossip magazines and tabloids. TarantulaGargantu is no longer part of the forum, so cannot be tracked down for further information, and his or her identity could be someone very close to Thomas.

The final version is the most low-key. It's that Thomas used his football earnings and made some smart property investments that returned him large profits. This is in line with girlfriend Kamila being in that industry, so she could have given him an introduction to its goings-on. He then reinvested, kept going and after a few years had built up the reported £100 million bankroll that he has now. This particular conjecture usually has the add-on that he used the comfort of that financial security to live in Vegas and while away hours playing poker, roulette and blackjack, which he is known to enjoy.

In a nutshell, no one really knows if Thomas has £100 million. If he has it, no one really knows how he made it. That's the charm of Thomas; you could believe any of the four theories offered as totally feasible for him to pull off. While it's unproven that he made that fortune, if he did, it seems most likely that it was at the card table. His 'big kid' nature would have made him a demon in a casino, as he wouldn't have felt any nerves or worry about the consequences, unlike most people. Forget weighing up odds, Thomas is bold enough to just go for it and not think about the ramifications – as his ex-team-mates are on record as confirming.

Danish football journalist Johan Lyngholm-Bjerge admitted, 'When he suddenly retired, he just disappeared.

When he did show up in Denmark, it was most often in his hometown Vejle and the club Vejle Boldklub. He has had the ability to just disappear even though he was one of our biggest stars. He's like a myth. Even his investments are like that. There are reports he's invested in all kinds of things and now has a big fortune, but we don't know for sure because he never says anything about them. That's Thomas.'

Archie Knox, Thomas's former assistant manager at Everton and the man who brought him to England, added, 'Nothing would surprise me with Thomas. Hearing about his life in Vegas, you'd go, "How the hell can you do that sort of thing? But he is a total one-off."

Very few footballers end up living a more glamorous life after they hang up their boots. So by whatever means he's done it, Thomas has gone on to do just that. Most of his peers disappear into normality but Mad Dog has turned into an international playboy, with the secrecy and a mystique that famed film character Keyser Söze from *The Usual Suspects* would be proud of. This seemed to be the way things would continue, with Thomas pursuing a champagne lifestyle as rumours swirled around him left, right and centre, with none being confirmed or denied. That was, until Thomas decided to break cover for a bizarre appearance, and speak publicly for the first time in 12 years.

Chapter 21

Invisible No More

AFTER shunning the cameras and any sort of profile since 2009, Thomas made a surprise appearance back on home soil. But it wasn't on a TV chat show or in a stage-managed piece to camera. Instead, he did a crossbar challenge on what appeared to be a kids' playground. Mad Dog faced off against Denmark ladies star Nadia Nadim in a filmed contest to promote bookmaker LeoVegas and its offers to customers for the upcoming 2018 World Cup in Russia.

For the uninitiated, the challenge is simple. The winner is whoever can hit a ball from outside the penalty box, smacking it directly off the crossbar the most times. It looks easier than it is as the flight and pace have to be spot on. Otherwise the ball sails over or dives down before it gets there.

So while Nadim managed to strike the bar once, giving her a 25 per cent success rate, Thomas effortlessly pinged four balls off the bar. Of course, it's only a small skill test but a decade after his retirement it backed up what all his previous team-mates had said, that he is blessed with serious skill levels. In the video, he doesn't compose himself; he rattles them off without even aiming. As he completes the last one, the microphones pick up Thomas screaming, 'Fucking four.' He's punching the air and marching around, proving that competitive fire is still in there – it probably won't ever be extinguished.

Another breaking of cover came after he was contacted by Ulrik le Fevre and his old club Vejle, and turned up to play in a friendly match. It was a squad of ex-professionals playing against a celebrity squad of musicians. Sometimes, players who've hung up their boots appear at these events with a paunch hanging over the waistband of their shorts, but not Thomas. He hit the field looking slim, trim and powerful. He looked like he did when he was playing at the top. Ulrik revealed that Thomas's mindset was still exactly the same as that of the 16-year-old kid who began his journey back in the 1990s. 'He was training very much and even before the benefit match, he'd trained for half a year. He was fantastic and the fans here love him.'

Being in Denmark for so long rekindled the interest of the media, as their golden goose was back in the fold. He hadn't jetted back to the US, as he normally did after a spell back home. Journalists and photographers were scurrying about on Gravesen watch. But something didn't add up.

Thomas lived his life according to a strict routine, like he'd always done. He would come home to Denmark twice a year, then head back to Vegas. This time he'd been in Denmark longer than normal. It wasn't like Thomas to just abandon his well-drilled way of operating. There had to be a reason.

As ever with him, nothing could be verified. Nevertheless, word had spread like wildfire, as in Thomas's case it's never presented in an official statement. The stories about him since 2006 had been a case of the media putting two and two together, crossing their fingers and hoping they got four. What was known was that Thomas had split from Kamila and left Las Vegas for good. He's now based permanently in Vejle, staying in his penthouse in The White Facet. There's no clue about how he's spending his days apart from local people seeing him around the town, where he is happy to chat away if stopped.

The good news is that he's smiling and appears to be happy. He's been spotted hanging out with old team-mates and pals Stig Tøfting and Niclas Jensen.

He's since started doing work as a pundit for Danish 6'eren TV, so fans can now hear his thoughts and analysis on the English Premier League. Speaking about his decision to join the station, which effectively meant he had gone from being a recluse to sitting in front of the nation on a weekly basis, Thomas said, 'Football fills a lot in my life and I've always done it. The euphoria has hit me again and I'm ready to become part of the high-level football world, this time on the sidelines as an expert. I would like to talk about football in a manner that is professional, but at eye level with viewers and supporters, because it is much more fun if they want to participate in the conversation.'

The only snippet of cast-iron personal news about Thomas came when he was snapped at his new friend Nadia's book opening standing next to a blonde woman. They could be dating. They could be friends. They might not even know each other. With no social media, no website, no PR representation, Thomas's world is impenetrable. The appetite for information about him was summed up by a picture in *SE og HØR* showing a gaggle of starved journalists around him with their recorders at the ready. At time of writing, however, the woman's identity is unknown.

Thomas chose to break his silence in an interview with Denmark's Kanal 5, a subscription station that broadcasts across the country. It's where Thomas settled a few scores about his career. Judging by his body language, he appeared relaxed and engaged but he was speaking about his favourite subject — football. Even if you don't speak Danish, it's clear he was happy to rattle on and share his views on all his old teams and discuss what he did in the game. Then, at the end, he cracked up in fits of laughter.

It was now relatively open season, well for him, on media access. Thomas agreed to an interview with football magazine *Tipsbladet,* again only speaking about the game. Below is a collection of his thoughts as they were reported in many media outlets around the world, with the quotes relevant to their location included. For example, his thoughts on Celtic were plastered across the Scottish sports pages. The thing is, as you'll see, there's no real insight. He wasn't pushed or asked about how he felt, how he functioned in a completely different way to other players, about how it feels to be a cult hero everywhere he's been, and not just for his football.

On Everton and his glory years: 'Everton took me in and gave me some amazing years of my life and my career. I was treated in a way that I am forever grateful for. I was not there for a long time to call it my club in my heart – that's Vejle Boldklub – but it was a great time. That was where I developed the most.'

On his days in Spain: 'It was a huge upheaval to go from the safe surroundings of Everton to this huge, giant club in a country where I could not speak the language. But they needed me and I had a role. And although it was a different role than the one I came from, I did it for the team's sake.'

On his fight with Robinho that ended his Real Madrid career: 'It was a normal day of training. I tackled him hard, and he did not like that. Then he hit me. I never caught him, fortunately.'

On the public's perception of his tough-guy persona on the pitch in Spain: 'It was the image and the reputation they thought I should have. I had no problems with people having their opinions. To me, it was about being honest with myself.'

On being frustrated at Celtic playing defensively: 'I've always been a Celtic fan. I saw the Old Firm game when Peter Løvenkrands played for Glasgow Rangers. I thought I would like to try to play in that atmosphere and I have not regretted that. Unfortunately, I ran into an obstacle in the form of a coach called Gordon Strachan. His time was unfortunately while I was there. It did not work between him and me. Gordon was a defensively oriented coach of a world-famous club. I remember that I scored a hat-trick against St Mirren and his only comment was, "Remember the defence."'

On being so combative on the pitch: 'If they were after my team-mates, they were after me too. It's always easier to break one player than a whole team.'

And that's it. It's dressed up by the old journalism black magic of pretending it's an exclusive and hard-hitting exposé after 12 years of *omertà*. But in reality, any supporter of any of the clubs Thomas was speaking about, or even a general football fan, would have known it all. Thomas hadn't broken cover, he'd just recapped what his Wikipedia page says. Members of the media were so desperate to hear anything from the Unicorn that they let their excitement get the better of them.

Why didn't they ask him about his £100 million and if he really had it?

Did he really lose a jaw-dropping $54 million in one game of cards in a Vegas casino?

Why did he quit so young?

Does he hate being a celebrity?

Would he rather have been a normal bloke and played football for fun?

Did he really bring dynamite into training at Hamburg?

Why did he spend his summers in a dark basement?

Well, they didn't ask him because Thomas wouldn't have answered. Why? Because he doesn't see those sorts of things as unusual.

He's not playing a character, he's a real maverick. Sadly, today, we're fed a stodgy diet of attention-seeking wannabes by all facets of the media. It's a shock when we're faced with the real thing.

And Thomas is that — he just happened to be a rich, gifted footballer, but that didn't make him a maverick. He was born that way.

Chapter 22

The Maverick

THERE'S nothing more tragic than unfulfilled potential. But the real tragedy is that many footballers self-diagnose, spouting off about how they could've gone to another level if circumstances had been different. They come out and criticise an old manager or blame their lack of maturity for not achieving a certain standard.

I frame that discussion in the context of Thomas Gravesen. You'd have to travel far and wide for someone to tell you that he was one of the best footballers in the world of his generation. You'll not see him exalted into the discussion alongside Zidane, Gerrard, Iniesta, Xavi, Pirlo, Nedvěd and Boban. But my feeling is that Mad Dog could and should have been in that heady mix, and the reason why he is not wasn't caused by his own failings. It was the failings of the commercially driven world of football and members of the industry who were unable to deal with someone who didn't fit their narrow interpretation of what a footballer should be.

Starting in his days at Vejle, Thomas was football obsessed and simply couldn't get enough of it. Not content to just go out and mess about with a ball, he adored the game. He had an unquenchable thirst for competition in order to test himself. Getting the bus to training, then leaving home at 17, he had a fire that was blazing. What separated Thomas from others who've failed to scale the heights that were expected of them was that he was willing to adapt if he believed in the plan, work hard and make the absolute most of everything he had. From a young age, he was wise enough to realise that you only get one shot and if you don't give it your all, you'll have to bear that cross forever.

That's why he has such respect for Fritsen and le Fevre. They recognised a kid with massive ability who was wired a little differently from the other boys. They sensibly took the approach that one size doesn't fit all. That's not to say they let Thomas get away with murder or turned a blind eye to his misdemeanours. That's another common trope from ex-pros that good managers cut maverick players slack and let them break rules because they are able to deliver match-winning contributions. That's not proper management. That's cowardice.

Fritsen told Thomas he wasn't being promoted to the first team as had been planned after he kicked out at another player in training. The rules were applied in the same way, but the communication was tailored so it connected with Thomas. If this pair of wise Danish veterans hadn't been so canny, then Thomas would have crashed and burned, and no one would ever have heard of him. Clearly, it was worth making the effort to get on Thomas's wavelength. After two years of professional football, he went to one of Germany's biggest clubs. If he'd been taken on by one of today's sanitised and calculating football academies, there's a good chance he would have been cut loose due to the obsession of many coaches with trying to develop carbon copies of the same profile.

Fritsen and le Fevre raised him but still allowed Thomas to be Thomas, and possibly without knowing it set the blueprint for how all his future managers should have acted if they wanted to extract his potential. Surely that's any superior's duty, to get the most from their subordinates and make the collective as effective as it possibly can be.

In Hamburg, Thomas showed he could cut the mustard. You don't go from playing in Denmark to joining a team like HSV and becoming an instant first choice unless you've got something about you. That was particularly true considering the German league was then such a combative arena, with only Bayern Munich lording it over the other teams. Everyone else had a puncher's chance of being up there alongside them. The thing that saved Thomas was that he was still young, so a lot of quirks would have been put down to that. Also, he was able to use his skill to convince

216

the coaching staff to push that to one side. It wasn't the right approach, but he left there intact probably because of his age; he hadn't been ground down.

Ironically, it was the other veteran pair of Walter Smith and Archie Knox who would save Thomas, as they realised what they had on their hands at Everton. A class act, but one who was unique, who didn't see things the same way as the rest of the squad. It takes an incredibly smart and insightful person to truly realise that not everyone sees things the same way. It's easy to say but in practice it's hardly ever displayed. Look at all the misunderstandings in romantic relationships that blow up into massive fallouts. They begin with a tiny incident that was down to two people seeing a straightforward situation differently. Well, Everton's Scottish duo had that insightfulness. They gave Thomas the confidence to be himself and at the same time realised he needed to be given a free role in the team. He had crazy fitness levels, passion in spades and mouth-watering skills. He just had to be unleashed.

Here, we can pick out a comparison with the one-time world's most expensive player Gareth Bale. He left Southampton as a raw teenager and moved to Tottenham Hotspur for an initial £5m, arriving as a defender, more specifically a left-back. In his first season, he was viewed as a flop, someone who was decent but not worthy of all the hype. It took manager Harry Redknapp to come in and use his undoubted talent for nurturing young players. He managed to get Bale engaged and realised that with the Welshman's physical capabilities he was actually a powerful left-winger. Fast forward to the 2018 Champions League Final in Kiev's Olimpiyskiy Stadium: Bale executes a jaw-dropping overhead kick to seal a third title in a row for Real Madrid and confirms that he's one of the best forwards on the planet. Without Redknapp having the nous to connect with him, Bale would still be playing in a position that he was good at, but well within his potential.

Another manager with a wise head was Morten Olsen, who was in charge of Denmark for most of Thomas's career. He was able to pair him up with Stig Tøfting and allowed Thomas to be himself. He did not make him feel that he had to rein it in. It's surely no coincidence that Thomas's spell in the team was a purple patch for Denmark. He wasn't a one-man team as there were several talented Danish players, but Thomas was the metronome who ran the show.

Just like Morten, Walter and Archie, forward-thinking David Moyes did exactly the same with Thomas at Everton. They all worked out what he had and deployed him in the best way for the team. It wasn't about them showing how tough they could be and refusing to allow him the freedom to express himself. Only someone with insecurities would do that. If trying to prove that you're more powerful than someone else overrides your overall perspective, then you've missed the point. Fabio Capello might have won a truckload of trophies but he bottled it and appeared lost when faced with Thomas. The guy trained like a bear; lots of figures go on record to confirm that. Thomas was driven and would run through brick walls. So why wouldn't you use someone of that nature in your team? Maybe it's because football has become so sanitised that players are marshalled and expected to be a herd of sheep. There's an image to follow and if you don't, you're out. A lot of the England international players spoke out after Capello left the job as national team manager about how he liked to march about and rule with an iron fist, making up rules that seemingly had no purpose. If you can play and train with the likes of Zidane, Figo, Raul, Owen, Beckham and Ronaldo and they give you praise, then you can certainly play. Thomas could play and he built up to a peak with Everton, leading them as a much more effective fulcrum than Wayne Rooney. It was Thomas's stewardship as the head man in that team that earned them their highest finish in the league. Maybe Capello struggled to handle such a complex character; he wanted a servant, not a general. Surely leading from the front and self-expression are qualities to be encouraged, particularly in top-level sport.

Then moving to Glasgow, Thomas and Gordon Strachan never appeared to be on the same wavelength. It didn't seem the Celtic manager wanted a maverick, so why did he sign Thomas? The spotlight at Real Madrid couldn't have been more intense. Every man and his uncle knew what Thomas was like on the pitch. Everyone knew he was a player who struggled to stick to a regimented role and would chase the ball with gusto. Maybe that was Strachan's issue, that Thomas refused to follow his instructions to the letter. The manager had proved with Southampton, by getting them to an FA Cup Final in 2003, that he had qualities, but it was always about being the plucky underdogs who kept their heads down and grafted hard for a brief moment of glory. It was different with Thomas. He was confident and would go out there with his chest puffed out to show what he had. To him, it was not about only playing the game, it was about inspiring everyone around you. They might not have his skill, but they'd see a team-mate expressing themselves and decide to have a go too. You might not always win, but would you rather live on your knees or die on your feet?

All the great work that had been done with Thomas was, for one reason or another, set ablaze and cast aside by Capello and Strachan. He wasn't acting up or being disruptive; that's just who he was. He was and is a maverick. His will to do well and play the game he loved was what made him get up in the morning. He was more committed than either of them assumed; they just didn't realise it. And their actions led to an unintentional but inaccurate media portrayal of Thomas.

It was the attitude from these two managers and the intense spotlight on his personal life that led to Thomas falling out of love with the game. The single thing that he lived for was taken from him and all the joy scorched. He was ground down. He was a big kid who just wanted to enjoy himself but the money, profile and egos meant he stopped smiling. That's why he retired so suddenly, only a few years after starring at the world's biggest club Real Madrid and disappearing into oblivion.

Roy Keane is, to my mind, the closest peer to Thomas. Keane was a marvellous player; he had a gift where he could channel the spirit of a team through him. He was able to absorb pressure and get even better. An individual like that was never going to be a yes man. That's why he was booted out of the Republic of Ireland's World Cup camp in 2002 and that's why he was driven out of Manchester United eventually. But did everyone think that his manner was an act?

Is it now so strange for someone to be the real deal and not just act a certain way on social media? Zlatan Ibrahimović does that. He puts on a persona and cashes in on it by doing cheesy adverts for Visa or taking out a full page in the *Los Angeles Times* telling the city that they're welcome, that he chose to play there. But many fans feel he couldn't lace the boots of Messi or Ronaldo. He's acting that way to garner more attention because his real personality can't. Did Beckham have to try so hard to get attention? Did Thomas have to go on TV to tell everyone he was a maverick? And just like them, Keane wasn't putting it on, either. They would all have been that way if they'd been milkmen or airline pilots. Meanwhile, a lot of columnists took the moral high ground and said it was the correct move for Sir Alex Ferguson to send Keane packing when he was kicked out of Manchester United.

To be a one-off, to be a loose cannon, is seen as a bad thing now in sport. That's what we've been brainwashed to believe. It's a good thing to be a nice, polite, respectful person, and it goes without saying, of course, that these are all admirable qualities. But anyone who stands out, doesn't wear the correct colour of socks or whatever else is then labelled a troublemaker. It's not their fault but so many athletes are one-dimensional. All they have is sport and there's nothing wrong with that. But for me, to be a true role model, you have to live on instinct and have a character that youngsters can look up to and almost touch. I don't want my sporting heroes to be living in safe mode because they need to protect corporate sponsorship or please a power-hungry manager. I want them to live how they feel and break down barriers.

Thomas Gravesen did that. He wasn't trying to be a maverick, he was one.

The tragedy was the homogenous world of football and its one-dimensional approach killed off Thomas's love for the game. He left aged 32 after a few scunnering experiences where he was made to feel that he wasn't welcome. He didn't fit in and no effort was made to help him. It wasn't down to rule-breaking or lack of ability – simply his personality wasn't being tolerated. When he played for a manager and club that took the time to understand him, the results did the talking. Did he improve Vejle, HSV and Everton? Yes. Did he impress and improve at Real Madrid? Yes.

So what about the big questions? Was there unfulfilled potential? Wasted talent? Absolutely — but it wasn't down to Thomas; he could only be himself. He simply wasn't given the opportunity to do so. Some quarters of football should hang their heads in shame as without cult heroes, without mavericks, without unique characters, we'd all be as well watching football played by robots.

Fans, young and old, want to be entertained, they want to feel that the players on the park are one of them. They want to watch people with imperfections. We've all got them and the perplexing thing is that football tries to airbrush them away. These are exactly the sort of characters who have made football the wonderful game it is.

With today's sanitised approach, commercial concerns becoming more and more important, and with many managers subscribing to the theory that no one should be treated differently, will we ever see another Thomas Gravesen?

Let's hope so. I'd take a player who adores the game, and can't believe they're playing in front of thousands every week, over some highly-trained academy graduate who's had all the individuality squeezed out of them, any day.

And if they don't do what everyone else does and if they are a maverick — well, even better.

Hold your head up high, Mad Dog, you did it your way.

Chapter 23

Mavericks United

HE wasn't the first but Thomas is the last of the great football mavericks. It's a long and interesting line. I'd like to pick out a few from down the years who've strolled into the game and kept their identity intact, no matter what the consequences.

A maverick is someone who's doing things because that's how they're wired; it's not a conscious choice and neither is it someone who isn't professional. So that's why I'd strike off one who's often called a maverick, George Best, dubbed the Fifth Beatle. He was adored by millions and was certainly a devastatingly good player for Manchester United as they won the European Cup in 1968, the first English club to do so. His close control was sublime and he'd jink past defenders as if they were treading water. Aside from that, a lot of what you'll hear about is his wild party lifestyle. The infamous tale that's been recounted many times is of the bellboy coming into his hotel room to find Best with a Miss World, lots of cash won in a casino lying splashed all over the bed and how he said: 'So George, where did it all go wrong?' To my mind, it didn't go wrong. Best maximised what he had. He became a top player and was just a guy who liked alcohol, and then sadly became addicted. It's not a trivial matter and it's a cruel illness that many people struggle with. But it doesn't make you a maverick.

So who are the true mavericks?

José Luis Chilavert

This colourful character was certainly one. He was labelled a South American revolutionary not seen since the days of Che Guevara. He was a Paraguayan goalkeeper who, as most fans will know, had a penchant for hitting free kicks. He wasn't too bad, either, and netted 46 goals in his career. He remains the only goalkeeper in top-flight football to score a hat-trick, which he did for Vélez Sarsfield in 1999.

Chilavert was in the game for 30 years, starting in the early 1980s, and had a fair degree of success. At the 1998 World Cup in France, he was voted into the All-Star squad. Riding high on that, he refused to play in the following year's Copa America, which was being held in Paraguay. It seems a nonsensical decision to turn down the chance to play in a home-based major tournament. Why? Chilavert felt that his government should not waste money by pumping it into a one-month sporting tournament. Instead, he felt it should go towards improving the country's education system. At the next World Cup in South Africa, Chilavert was banned from the opening game for spitting at Roberto Carlos during a clash with Brazil. On the surface, it was put down to the actions of a man with a bad temper. But Chilavert justified his response by claiming he was the victim of alleged racial slurs. Commenting on it, as reported by *The Guardian* and Sky Sports, he said: 'At the first corner kick, after he was called for a foul, this dwarf shouted to me: "Get up, Indian." After that, when they scored he touched his genitals to provoke me. When the match was going to end he pointed to the scoreboard and when the game ended and we were going to greet each other he told me: "Indian, we have won 2-0, you are a disaster" and he hit me. That's when I defended myself and I spat at him. Everyone in football knows that Roberto Carlos is a provoker. He always does the same and after that he does not recognise his mistake, and says he is innocent.'

Chilavert lived on his own terms and wasn't wrapped up in protecting an image that he could monetise or making sure he kept a place in the team. That was certainly the case in 2002, when the Paraguayan press waged a campaign against the appointment of manager Cesare Maldini. Chilavert rapped, 'About 90 per cent of sports journalists in Paraguay are incompetent.' Then, while in retirement, during a co-commentating job, he let rip at Paraguay's then manager Ramon Diaz and the football association. 'Failing began from the executives. They can't keep a coach who, in a year and a half and 19 games played, has only beat Jamaica, Venezuela and Bolivia. Díaz is an office clerk. He just closes himself, along with his son, in his office at the federation. His son was a poor and mediocre soccer player and he's the one who plans every soccer aspect of the team. But it's the executives' fault for paying a huge amount of money to someone who doesn't want to work.'

You can agree or disagree with Chilavert's opinions and his method of expressing them. But he was being himself; he was not saying something to get a pay cheque, as so many ex-footballers do when they become mouthpieces for their former clubs, peddling the party line.

Eric Cantona

King Eric — as he was anointed by his fans — stunned football when he announced his shock retirement aged 30. It wasn't injury-induced, or even due to a lack of success. He was at the peak of his powers after rejuvenating Manchester United and being part of back-to-back English Premier League victories for the Old Trafford club. He came to England initially for a trial at Sheffield Wednesday and then a short spell at Leeds United, where he won his first league title, playing 15 times. Cantona had been through a plethora of teams in France as a result of his chequered disciplinary record. He had thrown the ball at a referee and been hauled before a committee to explain his actions, where he accused them all of being 'idiots'. It was Sir Alex

Ferguson who spotted that he had that spark and ability that could inspire a team. He was able to connect with him, took the time to understand him and, in return, Cantona changed the club, and not just on the pitch. All of the Class of '92, as they're known — Ryan Giggs, Paul Scholes, David Beckham, Nicky Butt, Gary and Phil Neville — speak about Cantona's regimented attitude to practising his skills, which rubbed off. Beckham, in particular, has eulogised about how Cantona would spend hours working on his free kicks, so he did the same. The results speak for themselves.

Cantona was always a spirit who could never be tamed. That was proved in 1995 when he jumped into the crowd at London's Selhurst Park to attack a Crystal Palace fan who had abused him after he received a red card. He got a deserved eight-month ban.

But he didn't return a different character. Not because he wasn't sorry or didn't see the error of his ways, but because he was just being who he was. Like the way he'd always play with his collar turned up or how he'd quote obscure poetry; none of it was an act. Nike caught on to this and despite his lack of a family-friendly image or striking good looks, they made him one of their poster boys. It saw him star in big-budget TV ads and plastered on billboards. Fans and ordinary punters lapped up King Eric's unique ways.

When he retired it was to pursue his other passion in life, acting. He's gone on to appear in a host of French movies, plus the Ken Loach-directed *Looking For Eric*, which was about how football and a charismatic player can enable people to escape the day-to-day drudgery of normal life.

Speaking about his leaving the game so young, Eric said, 'When you quit football it is not easy; your life becomes difficult. I should know because sometimes I feel I quit too young. I loved the game but I no longer had the passion to go to bed early, not to go out with my friends, not to drink, and not to do a lot of other things, the things I like in life.' In a nutshell, he wasn't leaving to make a statement. He simply wanted to do something else and followed his heart, like any true maverick would do.

Brian Clough

One of the older examples is Brian Clough. He's fondly remembered as a manager but had a formidable scoring record as a player for his hometown team Middlesbrough. He netted 197 league goals in 213 appearances from 1955 to 1961. He went on to Sunderland, where his return was an impressive 54 in 61. The one glaring thing on his record is the lack of international exposure. He only played twice for England. That was the first indication that he didn't quite fit the predetermined profile. In those days, squads were heavily influenced by a panel of selectors, and managers were under more behind-the-scenes pressure to select the 'right' sort of characters.

Clough was clearly a man who knew his own mind. He got his first manager's job aged 30 at Hartlepool United.

The club were so poor that he got a licence to drive the team bus in a bid to save money. One year into the job, he was dramatically sacked, but reinstated following a boardroom coup. Clough then moved to Derby County, who were in the Second Division. He got them promoted and then won the First Division (now the Premier League) three years later. That was a staggering achievement for a provincial club. But it pales into insignificance compared with what he did at Nottingham Forest. He won the old First Division league title in 1978 and then back-to-back European Cups in 1979 and 1980, which was phenomenal. Very few teams have conquered Europe in successive years; it takes a great amount of tactical nous and preparation. If any English manager did that now, they'd be nailed on for a knighthood.

To win on that scale with limited resources at smaller clubs is a clear indication that Clough was doing things his own way. He wasn't following the same blueprint as everyone else. Before moving to Forest, he sampled life at a traditionally bigger club, Leeds United, and was sacked after 44 days when his distinctive manner didn't sit well with the star players and the boardroom hierarchy. That episode has since been turned into a movie, *The Damned United*, starring Hollywood leading man Michael Sheen as Clough. For similar reasons, Clough was also never given a chance to manage England, which robbed football fans of what would have surely been a great spectacle of Clough being in charge of the top players in the land.

Clough was an uncompromising character in everything he did, and it cost him opportunities and exposure. Again, that was only because of the risk-averse and narrow-minded climate he was part of. He would never have dreamed of changing to propel himself to a bigger platform, because like all the rest he wasn't choosing to be maverick. It's who he was.

Matt Le Tissier

The polar opposite of Clough is the player known as Le God. He was so laid back that nothing seemed to faze him. It's undoubtedly one of the reasons he only ever missed one of the 48 penalties he took at the top level. While it's an easy skill for a footballer, doing it in a game situation with pressure and expectation is why so many struggle and panic. Le Tissier never did. He played the game like a schoolboy, as is evident when looking back at some of the stunning goals he scored in England's Premier League, including his 1995 Goal of the Season, when he twisted and turned against Blackburn Rovers before cracking home a 25-yard screamer. His game was all delicate flicks, smart passes and controlling the ball like it was attached to his boots.

He was accused or lacking a big-time mentality because he was a one-club man. He played all his days at Southampton, making over 400 top-flight appearances. So again, we see the same pattern; you don't do what most other people do, so something must be wrong with you. No, something is wrong with you if you do things because everyone else thinks it's a good idea.

Le Tissier was happy and revelled in playing in a particular environment. The buzz for him was being a footballer and enjoying it. It wasn't about winning trophies or playing in front of the biggest crowds, he had other priorities and he stuck to them. The irony was that virtually all of the dissenters and people passing comment on him couldn't do a tenth of what he could with a ball. If being a footballer is about the game, then surely Le Tissier was the best of the lot.

Robin Friday

This maverick was a classic case of someone living in the moment, regardless of the consequences. Rock band Super Furry Animals even used a picture of Robin as the artwork for their 1996 single 'The Man Don't Give a Fuck'. He was a striker who played for Reading in a short-lived three-year glory period. Before becoming a footballer, he'd left school and been locked up aged 16 for theft. While he was in the borstal, he played for the football team and scouts noticed his talent.

Even playing for amateur sides after that, he regularly went AWOL due to drink and drugs. One time, he turned up so late for a match that by the time he got there, the clock showed 80 minutes. But he still came on to score the winner.

Reading eventually signed him on a pro contract in 1974 but their manager admitted he didn't fit in at training. 'Robin trained like he played, he had no other way of playing,' he said. His drinking carried on but he was such a good player that he was still selected and kept on producing performances. He was involved in numerous odd incidents, including walking into a hotel carrying a swan and even going to a nightclub in a long fur coat and hobnail boots before ditching the coat to reveal he was totally naked and continuing to dance proud as punch.

Eventually, he packed in football and worked as an asphalter and decorator. There was a petition with 3,000 signatures for Reading to re-sign him. The manager did try and told Friday that if he focused and did what he was told, then he could play for England. Friday replied, 'I'm half your age and I've lived twice your life.' He had another spell in prison for impersonating a police officer and died aged 38 from a heart attack. A book later claimed it was a suspected heroin overdose.

Friday lived on his own terms and wasn't chasing a dream; he played football because he loved it and was good at it. There's nothing wrong with having massive ambition in the game and wanting to win trophies and go to World Cups. But some players don't care about that. They want to go out, get on the ball and express themselves, scoring spectacular goals, pulling off long passes or whatever else that quickens the pulse of fans. With today's insistence on academies and career-orientated professionalism starting before kids are even teenagers, will we ever see anyone like Friday again? Let's hope so, as the game would be a lot better for it.

Thomas Broich

Another element regarded as dangerous in football is academia. There's a stereotype that most footballers are thick and lack intelligence. Beckham and Rooney are two prime examples of players who've been tarred with that brush. While it's resented, anyone who appears to be the opposite and have a wide variety of interests, or is considered an academic, gets pilloried as an oddball. This happened to German charismatic midfielder Thomas Broich. He came through just after the millennium at Borussia Mönchengladbach. His rounded personality automatically put some quarters of the game on red alert, as he didn't fit the profile of a footballer whose only pastime was playing video games and golf.

Thomas was into literature and classical music. He described football as an applied art. That led to the nickname Mozart, which stuck throughout his career, often patronisingly. His style of fluid play ran into problems when he was managed by Dutchman Dick Advocaat, whose own nickname, the Little General, says it all; a free spirit was never going to flourish under a coach with that moniker. Thomas did play under other managers but there always seemed to be this issue bubbling under the surface. He was easily one of the most creative midfielders in the Bundesliga but never got a full cap for Germany. By 28, he was considering quitting the game. What saved him was a move to Australia, where he joined Brisbane Roar and went on to play 181 times for them. Granted, it was a step down in level, but he was allowed to be himself without all the baggage. Down Under, football doesn't have the same engrained history as it does in Europe. There weren't any hang-ups on a footballer who liked to read or enjoy studying philosophy. Thomas said, 'I somehow had the feeling that they're all so scared in the Bundesliga. Every player is scared that they'll take something away from him.' That says it all; mavericks aren't out there protecting a manufactured image, they're letting it flow. It's the game of football that decides to get in the way and refuse to allow any expression to shine through, for fear of someone eclipsing the norms.

Graeme Le Saux

Another player who was lashed with the intellectual stick was the English full-back Graeme Le Saux, who was born on Jersey, one of Britain's Channel Islands. Scandalous rumours about his sexuality were allowed to float around the game for years, as if being homosexual was something to be ashamed of. For the record, Le Saux was married to a woman and had children, but that wasn't the point. It got so bad that Liverpool's Robbie Fowler bent over during a game and began pointing at his backside. Fowler also reportedly made a comment about how even Elton John was married. Fowler has since publicly apologised. The fact that Le Saux read the left-wing newspaper *The Guardian* was another common jibe, as if having different interests from most other players was a reflection of his ability. Le Saux had a distinguished career, winning the league at Blackburn Rovers and the UEFA Cup Winners' Cup with Chelsea, along with being a regular for England. But you can only wonder without the jibes and pressure, much of which the public wouldn't have seen, could he have been better? Even with his impressive performances and wand of a left foot, the most important thing Le Saux left behind was an example to kids: be yourself and if others can't handle it, too bad.

Romario

Untouchable confidence was something that the pint-sized Brazilian striker had in abundance. He won everything in the game: the World Cup in 1994, La Liga with Barcelona the same year and a hat-trick of Dutch leagues with PSV Eindhoven. Plus, he also scooped the Copa America twice during his glittering career. While he excelled, he was always a little different from the rest of his peers. His manager in Holland, Guus Hiddink, said: 'If he saw that I was a bit more nervous than usual ahead of a big game, he'd come to me and say: "Take it easy, coach, I'm going to score and we're going to win." What's incredible is that eight out of the ten times he told me that, he really did score and we really did win.'

At the height of his powers as the reigning FIFA Player of the Year, Romario walked out of Barcelona after an argument with manager Johan Cruyff. It's a recurring theme with mavericks; they stand their ground as they can only do it one way. It's not an act to get attention or to earn more money. Romario embodied that; he carried himself with a confidence and a respect for what he did. Disagreements with managers continued before he attacked a fan while playing in Qatar for Al Sadd after he threw live chickens at him. He'd spark off in these situations in a volatile manner, not because he was undisciplined or unruly, but because he felt an injustice had occurred and he had an innate drive to correct it. Being principled doesn't fit well in the modern game.

Admirably, Romário carried that exact same attitude into his post-football career in politics. He was elected as part of Brazil's Socialist Party in 2010, four years before the biggest spectacle in football, the World Cup, was due to be held in Brazil. It would be a perfect chance to promote himself. Being a global legend of the sport would really boost his political profile and allow him to climb the ladder.

So what did he do? He came out fighting against the whole concept of hosting it, denouncing it as being mired in corruption and money laundering. He went public and shouted from the rooftops, 'FIFA got what it came for: money. They don't care about what is going to be left behind. They found a way to get rich on the World Cup and they robbed the people instead. This is the real shame. You see hospitals with no beds, you see hospitals with people on the floor. You see schools that don't have lunch for the kids. You see schools with no air-conditioning, where kids are going to school in 45 degrees Celsius. You see buildings and schools with no accessibility for people who are handicapped. If you spend 30 per cent less on the stadiums, they'd be able to improve the other things that actually matter.' But he couldn't prevent it. Still, he fought the cause with the same vigour he would have showed during a tactical disagreement in his playing days.

In 2014, Romário was elected to the Brazilian senate with the most votes ever received by a candidate representing the state of Rio de Janeiro. He continues to be active in politics at time of writing. He's the same geezer, whether he's in a pair of boots or dressed in a suit.

Sócrates

This Brazilian genius is another member of Mavericks United who marched to the beat of his own drum. He was known as 'The Doctor' thanks to having a medical degree, but still smoked and drank prodigiously throughout his playing career. He was a technically gifted playmaker who captained Brazil at the 1982 World Cup and then appeared at the following tournament in Mexico in '86. He was a very tall man, two-footed and with an eye for goal. Sócrates was regarded as the brains of the teams he played in. While a lot Brazil's players rise out of poverty, Sócrates grew up in a well-off family and had access to a wide range of free-thinking books. One day as a child, he watched his father destroy them all. The reason was that the country was in the midst of a *coup d'état* and he would have been accused of being against the new regime if he'd kept them. This incident stuck with Sócrates – who died in 2011 – but only made sense in later life.

While playing for Corinthians, he co-founded Corinthians' Democracy, which was a challenge to Brazil's military dictatorship. He wanted the club to stop ruling the players with authoritarian vigour. Sócrates led votes for the players on matters such as what time they wanted to eat lunch or whether they wanted to spend the night before matches in a hotel.

He even laid down an ultimatum in 1984 by coming out in support of Diretas Já, a popular democratic movement, and vowed that if it didn't succeed, he'd leave Brazil. A media report stated, 'Sócrates took the risk of saying, in front of two million people gathered on the cathedral square, that if direct presidential elections weren't accepted by the regime, he'd go play in Italy.' It did lose and he moved to Florence to continue his career. This proved to all that he viewed basic lifestyle conditions above football or his own goals as an athlete.

After his career was done, Sócrates went on to practise medicine and revealed who his three childhood heroes were — Fidel Castro, Che Guevara and John Lennon.

When was the last time a modern footballer named those type of figures as inspirations? And that's what being a maverick is all about. There's no shame in being different.

Chapter 24
The Fans

FOOTBALL is played for the fans. Without them, regardless of riches, exposure and commercial deals, the game wouldn't mean anything. So bringing this book to a close, I'll let the people who've watched Thomas strut his stuff over the years offer their memories of him.It's apt as Mad Dog was always one of them. No matter what level he reached or what stadium he played in, he never changed. He was a fan who happened to find himself out on the pitch.

Jens Flø, a lifelong Vejle Boldklub fan.
'Probably due to my age, I don't have one overriding memory of Thomas. I remember him being the biggest star of a very young and talented Vejle team. Mostly, I remember his amazing character. A man with huge drive that had to be managed, but as I see it, his drive was also what made him the player he was.

'The ending of his career and his decision not to speak with the media was found strange by many people. I don't think it has damaged his legacy, though. In Vejle, he is a legend and a person that everyone loves. He is loved for his character. He still claims his love for Vejle Boldklub and regularly shows up for games. Thomas is not only a legend in Vejle, but in all of Denmark.'

Tom Martin, ex-Everton season ticket holder in the top balcony at Goodison and also a programme seller. Now lives in France and follows the team from there.
'I was eight when Tommy came to Everton. I had a season ticket the whole time he was with us, so watched him a lot. I loved singing "Tommy Tommy Tommy Tommy Gravesen" at the top of my voice, even when others around me saw it as unfit.

'I just remember enjoying watching him play and always following him, even without the ball, to see if he was going to do something crazy. I can remember little things, like when he "attacked" Carsley while waiting for kick-off, or when he hurdled the hoardings so he could get a long enough run-up when taking a throw; they were just typical Gravesen moments. He was a hero.

'His legacy is a strange one. There is a definite split right down the middle of the fan base as to how people remember Thomas. For fans like me, I loved every minute Gravesen was at our club. Yes, he was a nutter, but a nutter you want

241

on your side. Someone who could make you laugh, cringe and wonder at his skill, all in the space of 90 minutes.

'For others, he was a mentally unstable liability who was all bravado and no substance. His wild side was something that put us in trouble more often than it gained us an advantage. Admittedly, he did cause us some bother at times. I always thought the nickname Mad Dog did him a disservice; he was much more than a wild hard man. He possessed more footballing ability than most in the Everton team. He could pick a pass, swing a cross in and pull out a silky trick from nowhere. In my opinion, his ruggedness prevented a lot of people from seeing the refined side of his game.

'When remembering Tommy, I think it's important to see past the modern obsession with sports science, statistics, and systems.

'Football is, above all, an entertainment business.

'On this count, Gravesen was one of the best. Win, lose or draw, he never failed to entertain the paying fans. Sometimes with a standout performance, often with a touch of brilliance, a crunching late tackle or a defence-splitting pass.

'And of course, more than the occasional "what the hell just happened?" moment.

'A gifted footballer, an unfathomable mind, and as far as I could tell, a complex but decent human being. All in all, a far cry from the characterless athletes that litter the game now. For that, I'll always remember with a smile Tommy's time with the Mighty Blues.'

Joe Cunningham, president of the Houston Bobby Lennox Celtic Supporters' Club.

'I was personally disappointed with Thomas, as when I heard we had signed him, I was over the moon. I thought he was a fantastic player and a great signing. It didn't quite work out for some reason. I'm still blown away that he didn't make it at Celtic. I've never understood that, I thought he would have been brilliant.

'I'm of the belief that most people were thinking the same as myself when we signed him – which was, brilliant.

'I don't believe he left any kind of legacy. I think everyone felt let down. We all had great admiration for him but for some strange reason he was a shadow of the player we thought we were getting.

'To this day I still can't get my head around it. He was a fantastic player before we got him; maybe Celtic are to blame.'

Pascual Llopis, Real Madrid socio for over 20 years.

'He put himself in the firing line in a difficult time when the team was crumbling little by little. He stood up to be counted. After that, he was unjustly sacrificed to bring others in with bigger names, who didn't make the team any better.'

Frankie McKay, of the Jim Craig Celtic Supporters' Club in Lurgan, County Armagh.

'I will always remember his first Old Firm game at Celtic Park, where he opened the scoring in a 2-0 win. His goal, coupled with Kenny Miller's first Celtic goal, were seen as important landmarks in hopefully kick-starting both of their Celtic careers. Both celebrated the goals and win as if they had totally bought into the Celtic family, and what these games mean to us supporters.

'Gravesen had been seen as the archetypal hard man in the engine room but also someone who possessed the experience and talent to go with being a renowned international player. His performances in the English Premiership with Everton, followed by a season at Madrid, where he played a serious amount of games, was the reason his arrival was seen as a major coup and signal of intent by the club that they were keen to sign the quality to lift the club to a new level.

'To score in an Old Firm win, in a season when Celtic won the league fairly comfortably, should always be sufficient to endear you into the hearts of the Celtic faithful forever.

'Thomas showed glimpses of the ability and qualities he undoubtedly possessed, but the disappointing thing was they were too infrequent. That said, he pulled on the hoops and contributed to some success at the club, and at Celtic he will always be seen as one of us, someone who had the opportunity to do what the majority of us supporters will never have the fortune to do — pull on the hoops, play at Celtic Park and lift a trophy for the club. His legacy will always be that in the record books of Scottish football, the SPL title in 2006/07 was won by Celtic and Gravesen contributed to that. No one can take that away from him and despite any ill feeling over his departure from the club, he will always be welcomed back at Celtic Park by the supporters.'

Tony Killen, Everton supporter who watches from the Upper Bullens Road Stand at Goodison.

'He was able to supply a touch of class to the Everton midfield at a time when it was conspicuous by its absence. I had heard how well he was doing at Hamburg and to be honest, was surprised there were not more English clubs interested in signing him. Perhaps his reputation for being somewhat unconventional in his approach was off-putting.

I have to say that for all the grimacing and gurning on the field, and tales of his pranks during training, I can't ever remember him being publicly in the doghouse for the way he behaved. That said, like many creative players, he always seemed to be someone whose contribution could be affected by his mood. He needed to be "up for it" to produce his best. When he was in the mood, however, his control, drive and passing ability were of a very high level.

'His partnership with Lee Carsley was an interesting one as they largely complemented each other. Thomas's signing for Real came out of the blue, and I can still recall them extolling his virtues as a hard-working, unflashy and reliable player who would be happy to undertake the "grunt work" in midfield on behalf of Galácticos, such as Zidane and Figo, but who would be happy for them to take the limelight.

'I was not the only Evertonian at that point to reckon that he had described the Carsley role to a T. It was from that point that we believed they had signed the wrong baldy. I'm still certain of it today, but I guess we'll never know for sure.'

Daniel Hartmann, Celtic fan from Dresden, season ticket holder in section 411.

'I had seen Thomas Gravesen playing many times before he came to Celtic as a child in Germany, and to me he was always a player I could only like if he was on my favourite team.

'He was known as a friendly, funny guy but on the pitch he always fought for every inch, and as a young boy I thought he was scary.

'When he came to Celtic, I was glad because he had so much experience and was not afraid of anyone. Exactly what we need when playing in the Champions League and against Rangers. My overriding memory of Thomas at Celtic is his first Glasgow derby. Gravesen and Neil Lennon were all over them in midfield and Gravesen even scored to make it 1-0. His celebration was so emotional; he just screamed and let it all out, which is what all of us supporters do when we score against them. This is what sticks out to me: his intensity and spirit. He seemed to be able to influence things by being such a big presence.

'Looking back now, it seems unbelievable to me that he played so few games for Celtic, because personally I felt that he really made an impact when he played and he was part of a team that won us the league by more than ten points.

'Celtic fans love players that play with high intensity and the way Gravesen performed and celebrated his goals in these derbies. It felt like he knew exactly what it meant to the Celtic support and in those moments when he celebrated, he was one of us.'

Peter McCann, loyal Everton fan who's attended every home game since August 1977.

'My memories of Tommy are of his great technical and passing ability. In all the time I've watched Everton, I've never known a player to divide opinion like him. He was like Marmite but unlike that product, I loved Tommy. I don't think I have seen an Everton team rely on one individual like the early David Moyes teams did on Tommy. When you get so much of the ball, there are going to be wayward passes but some people couldn't see that. I wish more people could appreciate what a top player he was.'

Miroslav Petrovic, Vejle Boldklub fan who still sees them play in his role as a football cameraman in Denmark.

'Thomas broke into the first team and was a big part of the team that came second in the Superliga in 1996/97. I was nine years old and was not a fan of VB. But the frenzy surrounding them at that time, and Thomas Gravesen especially, got everyone's attention. So when my father asked me if I wanted to go to a game during the spring of 1997, I was not hesitant. It was a packed Vejle Stadium and even though I was sitting on my father's shoulders, I could not see a thing on the pitch. By the time the match had ended, I was hooked. The atmosphere, the sounds, everything about the experience had me excited. During that spring season, I watched a couple of games at the stadium with my dad and during the summer vacation, I was determined to go back and see another game the following season. That game just so happened to be where Gravesen's departure from VB to Hamburg was announced. I remember him receiving giant applause. I had no idea who he was. But I knew that I wanted his autograph. I was wearing my Danish '492 European Championships top, which was a Flemming Povlsen number nine jersey. It was the only red jersey I owned and I wanted Gravesen to sign it. When he came up to the stands and greeted all the people, some of us kids got right in front and asked for his autograph.

'I remember turning around so he could sign the back of my shirt, and when he saw what I was wearing he said, "I'm just gonna sign it here, above Povlsen." I think that says a lot about his mentality; even though he was just 21 years old and about to play for another club than his childhood team for the first time, he felt he belonged above Flemming Povlsen."

'My passion for football was lit during that period, and as a proud supporter of VB, following Gravesen's career was the most natural thing. During his stints at Everton and especially Real Madrid, I saw as many games as I could on TV.

'In the eyes of VB fans, I know Gravesen is definitely one of the all-time greats, and for my generation maybe the greatest. Allan Simonsen will always be one step ahead because of his honours during his career, most notably the Ballon d'Or in '77, but that was before my time. I have great respect for the players that established VB's reputation in Danish football as a technical team. But for me, Gravesen and the 1996/97 team stand above all. Gravesen's legacy with the fans is one to be proud of. Whenever a player joins the team and plays in midfield, he is expected to live up to the stature and the demeanour of Gravesen. Always giving it his all, always tackling with courage and being a leader. I think that is what fans remember about Gravesen, his attitude and his willingness to sacrifice everything for the team. We don't always remember that he was an excellent technical player. What stands out was his fierce style and no-nonsense attitude."

Brian Wilkinson, Everton diehard who regularly sits in the Park End at Goodison.

'My overriding memory of Gravesen was as part of a double act we liked to call the Mitchell brothers, due to the resemblance to Grant and Phil Mitchell from the BBC soap *EastEnders*. To be honest, I think I would have preferred to come up against Phil and Grant, rather than Tommy and Lee Carsley. Both took no prisoners on the football pitch. With Tommy, though, he could run through an entire team, had great vision and very rarely came out second best.

'You always had a chance when Gravesen turned up; you could sense the fear in the players when he gave his stare. His crazy eyes struck the fear of God into the other players, and that was only his own team-mates. Who knows how the opposition felt?

'He had so much talent and a will to win, even today he is still talked about as a player with fire in his belly, who would give his all for both the club and the Evertonians.

'Gravesen arrived at the right time when players could still make a tackle without being penalised. I'm not sure if his hard-but-fair tackles would stand up now as the game is heading closer to a non-contact sport.'

Daniel Busch, HSV fan.

'My overriding memories of Gravesen are his sense of humour and his relentless style of play. He was always up for a joke or a prank, which earned him the nickname

Humörbombe in Hamburg. Despite his young age, when he arrived, Gravesen was quickly a leader on the pitch and immediately earned respect with his hard-working approach. He was also famous for his craziness on and off the pitch, which made him feared by team-mates and opponents.

'You won't find an HSV fan who has a bad word to say about Gravesen. He is loved for his humour and honest approach on the pitch and is a cult figure in Hamburg. Many people were proud when he signed for Real Madrid after starting his European career in Hamburg. He is a hero and a legend to most HSV fans.'

James Hughes, Everton supporter.
'He was a crazy, unpredictable talent with one hell of an eye for a pass and was more of a playmaker than many credited him as. My best memory was his contribution in the 2004/05 season before sealing a move to Madrid. He played his best football and galvanised the team with match-winning performances. His legacy was he was a major reason that we finished fourth that season, such was his fine form in the first half of that season, and for that he'll always be remembered.

'His return to Everton in 2007 on loan proved to everyone Tommy was a Blue at heart. I would say the vast majority of Everton fans look back fondly and appreciate that we got the barmy Dane at his best.'

Sources

This book is based on my interpretation and a series of personal interviews I conducted with various people. I am grateful for their cooperation in this project.

For other quotes, information, statistics and match reports, I have consulted and used:

BBC Sport
The Daily Record
The Daily Mirror
The Guardian
The Independent
The Daily Mail
The Telegraph
Liverpool Echo
The Sun
Al Jazeera
Marca
El Pais

SOURCES

Bild

B.T.

Tipsbladet

Kanal 5 (Denmark)

SE og HØR (www.seoghoer.dk)

Euroman (www.euroman.dk)

Vice Sports (https//sports.vice.com)

FourFourTwo (www.fourfourtwo.com)

Sky Sports (www.skysports.com)

MLS Soccer (www.mlssoccer.com)

The Premier League (www.premierleague.com)

Open Goal (www.open-goal.co.uk)

ToffeeWeb (www.toffeeweb.com)

UEFA Champions League (www.uefa.com)

GrandOldTeam (www.grandoldteam.com)

253

Index